Keep the flames burning

Save your relationship before it´s too late!

60 Tips that work

Emily Sophia Johnson

thanks to

christian and jens

who made it all possible

Disclaimer and Terms of Use: Effort has been made to ensure that the information in this book is accurate and complete, however, the author and the publisher do not warrant the accuracy of the information, text and graphics contained within the book due to the rapidly changing nature of science, research, known and unknown facts and internet. The Author and the publisher do not hold any responsibility for errors, omissions or contrary interpretation of the subject matter herein. This book is presented solely for motivational and informational purposes only.

First Edition: July 2014

ISBN-13: 978-1500646721

INDEX

PREAMBLE

Relationships are complex constructs. Often people experience severe difficulties in maintaining their relationships properly. With time feelings fade away. While researching for this book I found out that most couples who experience severe problems cannot even tell exactly what caused them. Before this state passes a point of no return, the common question is "What can we do to fix this?". Possible consequences of not doing anything are boredom, mutual ignorance and disinterest and most couples will likely part ways. Asking the question what was missing to have a fulfilling and loveful relationship, the most common answers where a lack of shared interests, beloved activities and desire for each other.

In this book, I am trying to give inspiration and deliver easy and actionable advice to those to are willing to take action. I'll show you how to re-ignite your relationship with just a few behavior changes. I'll explain how to earn new trust and which steps to take in order to prevent your relationship from failing. I will show you to avoid relationship killers which sneak into your everyday life.

In this book I am going to show you 60 specific ways to keep the flames burning. Be it friends, private environment, work or your family - each of those are factors that contribute to the success or failure in a relationship. With my advice you get tips on how to use each of these factors to strengthen and stabilize your relationship.

I hope this book helps you to prevent problems and to overcome obstacles. Remember, what stands in your way, becomes the way – don’t let your love fade away.

I wish you a happy relationship.

Sincerely Yours,

Emily Sophia Johnson

MOVIE NIGHT

Movies indisputably play an important role in people's lives. We do not only watch films to be entertained but also because we relate to the stories in them. Yes, some movies parallel my life story. They can mirror yours as well. And they have been showing us important things about ourselves for decades now. The genres range from horror movies to comedies, from war films to drama pieces, from fiction to documentaries. Our lives can fluctuate between those same planes. Cinema is indeed like a blueprint not only of our experiences but also of our dreams. Often, we find ourselves watching movies because we share the same dreams as the characters. Undeniably, movies influence us.

Speaking of cinema as being like our own portrait, we often think of inviting our loved ones to a certain movie to let them see who we are. Cinema has been used as a tool for sharing.

Here you are, very excited to invite your partner. You think this is silly because you've been together for a long time, but you are wrong. Spending some time watching movies together is not only for newer couples; it's for everybody, even for friends. This is because films create a certain effect on those who watch together.

The first thing to do is to check what movies are playing. It is good to consider this before inviting your partner. Every movie tells a different story, so choose something to which both of you can relate. Although not much of it will fit you both perfectly unless it's a true-to-life story about your relationship, the important thing is to choose a story that will take you and your partner on a journey where love is strong. Press that ignition button.

The second step is to connect to your partner. Connecting means to make them feel that you are not just sitting beside them but also that you are sharing the same thoughts about what you are watching. For instance, if the man in the movie shows care and devotion to his love, then touch your partner's hand, look into their eyes and smile. It is simple, but it says, "Hey, I also care for you."

With things like this, you have to consider not only your own interests but your partner's too. Think of the role that cinema plays in our lives. Going to the movies has been described as a way of exploring your personality. So watch the signs from your partner and then connect. It is a fresh, "on-field" activity that will surely unwind both of you.

MONTHLY DINNER DATE AT DIFFERENT RESTAURANTS

They say the way to a man's heart is through his stomach, and to some extent this is true with women's hearts too – just like doing things to "impress" not only works on women but on men as well. To keep the flame burning in a relationship, going out and having dinner with your partner is a good idea. In that environment, you will be able to talk and act as if you are just getting to know each other or getting better acquainted. Dinner dates are exciting, but dining in a different restaurant once a month is a lot more exciting.

If you want to go out to eat, then do it in the most delightful and fun way. Delightfulness does not always come with a price. It is enough that you explore different restaurants as options. They say every eating establishment has a different aura. Let that aura flow. It will not bore you or your partner.

In deciding between one restaurant and another, there are several things to consider. First, choose a restaurant that interests both of you without settling for the usual kind of food you eat at home. If dining at a seafood restaurant is unusual for you, then give it a try. Second, keep the location a secret but give your partner a hint as to what kind of place you are going to – casual or formal. That way your partner can dress appropriately. Third, it is important that you don't visit the same kind of place every month. Change from a seafood place to a candlelight dinner to a food truck to a pop-up restaurant. Why? This shows that you are exerting thoughtful efforts to plan new and exciting culinary excursions. Finally, the fourth thing you must think about is comfortability. It is good to shift to a restaurant that is very different from the one you visited last month, but don't go to extremes that would make your partner uncomfortable. If, on the other hand, you know that they wouldn't mind a bit of discomfort, then be daring.

The critical thing with this activity is to put both of you in a new environment together. It will bring out the different shades of your personalities. Loving, fun, carefree, romantic, thoughtful, and adventurous traits, to name a few, will surface. These will become the highlight of every dinner you and your partner share. If you have lost sight of the romance that thrilled you in the past, this will help rekindle your love by reminding your partner that the two of you had once upon a time enjoyed each other's company, and you can once again, and for the rest of your days.

Dining out need not always be formal. Formality does not help when things in the relationship are a little bit rocky. It only brings the same superficiality you have shared together for the last years, the very thing you wanted to get rid of. Learn to loosen up.

ROMANTIC DATES

Has your relationship grown boring lately? You might need to reconnect. Reconnection is a form of communication in which couples are brought back to their former state of happiness and unity. The reconnection process, here, is likened to a reconnection in a magnetic field wherein two factors will be drawn together into the same magnetic line from different magnetic fields. To change to a different magnetic field means a lot of force may be needed. Your connection may have been lost as one of you strayed to a different field. Though, generally, it is believed that people come from different fields, the moment you come together as one, you have already crossed over to the same field. Unsuccessfully, you fail to stay on that field for very long. Another tip for reconnection is going on romantic dates.

Step #1: Recreate the days when you were in love or burning with lots of passion for each other.
In this step, it is suggested that you repeat the first day you met each other. Remember your first words to each other and say them even if it they are not expressions of love.

Usually, the people we have ended up falling in love with are the ones we least expected to be "the one" at the very outset. It is normal that our first words were not expressions of love.

Step # 2: Replay your first date or the time where you first fell in love.
Most experts on relationships recommend this activity. Due to its proven positive effect, those who have been to marriage counseling have been advised to do this. Remembering how your first date was will stimulate old feelings. Don't worry if it was awkward. Awkwardness sometimes can be sweet. You might share a big laugh remembering that awkwardness.

Step # 3: Change your views.
The reason that coldness between you and your partner exists is because as time goes on, you move into a different field of views. No matter how small the change is, it can create a gap in the relationship. Changing your views on things, and finding a middle ground for both of you, definitely can rekindle the fire. Share the same views. Then go for romantic dinners, when all of these three steps are established.

The thing about romantic dinners is that they can be too sweet or too corny. It is important that you not overdo your plan. Some people spend hundreds of dollars to impress their partner and call it romantic. That is not necessarily true. You can't go into romantic mode when you and your partner are not both feeling in that mood. The purpose here is to help you rekindle the love that you used to have, and an automatic candlelight dinner with a parade of music can't create that magic automatically.

ROMANTIC WEEKEND TRIP

You wanted to test a relationship, see the sights and enjoy new places together. You wanted to impress your partner, and so you chose to travel. You still want to keep the relationship alive, so why not travel together again?

We often think of travelling when we accomplish something worthy of celebrating. We go on vacation to a place we've been eager to visit for the last 6 months. You think it might be healthy for you and your partner to get away. You are right. But if the purpose is to keep the relationship strong, it might be better to go on a small yet romantic weekend getaway rather than a long and far vacation that you can afford only once every 2 years. The problem is how to make this weekend trip work.

The first thing to do is to be realistic. You are not perfect, and you can't be. Another sure thing is that your partner is not either. So be true to yourself. Don't go beyond what is reasonable; that means don't expect too much out of the situation. Don't overdose on romance hormones. Here are the top suggested romantic weekend trips for you and your partner.

•A concert. Yes, invite your partner to a concert even if it is not a ballad concert and both of you feel out of the age bracket. Concerts can put you and your partner into the mood. Who would not be when everyone around you is in love and taking in the moment?
•Enjoy some time at a resort. Make reservations at a place that is beautiful and interesting. You'll have a lot of time to forget the hectic world, which is the first step. Once you have reached that level of peace, you can create new things with your partner. Reconnect to your love while disconnecting from everyday life.
•Sail. Sailing is a naturally romantic activity. You feel the free air, the smell of the sea, and feel your partner while you're somewhere alone together. Everything else will be eclipsed next to the city lights and the stars. This does not necessarily mean taking a cruise. Just riding on a yacht or a boat is enough to turn these effects into reality. This activity is perfect and must be done naturally, and you must be skillful.

These tips, like any other tips, depend largely on the participation of the couples. If your partner does not plan these activities with you, then there is a good chance that you may able to fix your relationship by impressing your partner by following these amazing tips. It would be a lot better, though, if the man initiates this activity. Your woman will surely cling to your arms just like before.

DAILY "I LOVE YOU" TEXT

Love letters even in these days are signs of admiration and love. They are the best and sweetest way of saying "I love you, " "I care a lot, " "I admire you, " and many more things. Love letters and notes, they say, are signs of puppy love. Well, the fact is that many puppy loves endure and create a certain feeling, which is unforgettable. The purpose here is neither to create puppy love nor to remind your partner about her puppy love. The purpose is just to help you do the things again that made your love unforgettable. On the other hand, love letters, as they say, don't come so easily anymore. Though I personally prefer love letters, let's go for a substitute. A very common thing that almost everybody does nowadays is texting. These two things, though done differently, convey a similar message. They communicate a person's thoughts and feelings.

Texting can be so magical. Have you ever heard of textaphrenia? They call it a disorder, but I call it a skill. Textaphrenia, as they define it, is a disorder when a person checks their phone every now and then because they imagine that they've gotten a new one or can feel the vibration of their phone ringing when it is actually not. The aim here is to spread this disease. It could be used to keep the love burning. How so? Here's how.

The key to this strategy is to text your partner a short, even nonsense message. What is important is that you text and your partner reads your message. Content is not necessary but, of course, don't text something that would make your partner angry, disappointed, or anything that would invite a negative aura. A simple "hi" could do, or a "good morning," or an "I hope you're okay." It is necessary that your text is able to be resent tomorrow. So do not text something that is an occasion-based message; with regards to this activity, you can send your partner another message. Having established what to text, you must also decide on when to send that message. For instance, your message says, "Snack already?" and you've been sending that at 3 p.m. daily. Nevermind the response. Or you might not get one. Make sure you sound like a busy man in your replies. The tip is to continue sending the message at the same time with the same message for at least 2 weeks straight or more, and then stop. Know what will happen? Your partner at 3 p.m. will check the phone. Unknowingly she will miss your text the next day, then the next day.

This strategy will make your partner think of you every day in the middle of the busy day.The moment you stop will make your partner miss you because she wanted to read your message, although she knew it would be the same one. The effect is great. You should make your other romantic moves at home then.

FLOWERS ON A REGULAR BASIS

Love depends on magic. The more sparks you feel for your partner, the sweeter your love will get. It takes some spark plugs to ignite that spark in your partner, and one of those is flowers. Both in the past and nowadays, flowers have been very meaningful for girls. A bouquet never fails to paint a smile on their lips. For a continuous and never-fading spark, you can buy her flowers on a regular basis.

The very purpose of this activity is to remind your partner how special she is to you, and flowers can help you do that.

Consider this as a scent to your blooming relationship. Girls normally become moody. You know why? They always want to be seen as special in your eyes. If this is what they want, then why don't you give them that feeling? To give these feelings, the formula is a stunning start plus an aftershock.

How can you best follow this tip? A stunning bouquet of red, fragrant roses will probably be perfect. Use her favorite color in the bouquet, and add a personalized message. It would be great if the number of roses signified something about your relationship. Let us say, 20 roses for your anniversary if you are celebrating your 20th or it falls on that day of the month. If your anniversary falls on the 9th or earlier in the month, which means fewer flowers, then switch to another occasion like the number of months you've been together. Compose the most romantic message that you can think of to show her that she is your greatest treasure of all. Remember that you can always add something when you give the flowers, such as chocolates and other gifts she will love to receive.

Why does this have to be on a regular basis? Regularity doesn't mean every day, but the more often it can be done, the better. After the stunning start that will shake her heart, don't forget the aftershocks to keep her shaking and falling for you. This will be great. For even greater opportunity to add more sparks, you should use variation with your flowers. Explain as sweetly and caringly as possible the message that you want the flowers to symbolize. Say, for example, *"Dear, after giving you all my heart with the red roses, please accept these white roses, for this is the sign of my pure intentions to you and my loyalty. These flowers will fade, but my loyalty never will; it will be forever yours. I love you."* Don't forget the magic words.

Giving flowers on a regular basis will surely help you, but as a real man, you should not only give her flowers, gifts and messages. You have to demonstrate the meaning of all of these things with your actions. You have to stand on your words. Flowers will be more special if they are given with all your love. Always remind your partner how much she means to you.

PLAY SPORTS TOGETHER

Today everybody knows how many benefits sporting activities may have on human health. What hasn't been understood so clearly is that sports can have amazing effects on a couple's relationship if they are practiced by the couple together. To play sports by yourself, alone, surely can be boring sometimes. You will not feel motivated. Just like in a relationship, sports do not motivate a player when he is alone. Sports require a companion, a partner who will be there to play with. Here are just a few of the reasons why you and your partner should decide to play sports together.

Studies have shown that people tend to copy the healthy habits of their partners. In fact, it has been found that sport activities initiated by a partner also help their partners to lose weight in a better manner than if they were to do it alone and individually. There are many other benefits of this activity.

If you're wondering what connection exists between sports and love, the answer is simple. There is a close connection between the two: when a person decides to get rid of some extra pounds, this means that he or she wants to look good for his or her partner. In this way, sport becomes a proof of love.

The first thing to do is to find out what are your partner's limits and preferences. By learning those, you can adjust to the things your partner can do. Doing extreme sports, usually based on your preference, will not make for a healthy relationship. The purpose here is to enjoy fun moments together and at the same time get great benefits for your health. You can go jogging, for instance, or maybe tennis would be a better choice for you and your partner.

Play sports together for an hour a day; this will definitely strengthen the relationship between the two of you. Science shows that doing a sport activity will increase the endorphins a body releases. This production of endorphins will significantly increase your libido. Then, over time, performing physical activities together will become a habit. Good things will follow, especially in hard times when the other partner lacks motivation to continue, the other one will provide the necessary power for the partner not to quit just like in every relationship. You have to nurture that feeling.

No matter what type of sport you play together, you will be amazed by the wonderful effects of this. Today people play sports for different reasons. They say it's for their health, to get rid of the excess pounds, and more. It's good for us to note that sports bring us closer to our loved ones. But for this to work for your relationship, both of you must possess the necessary will, because if it is missing, you will not get very far. Motivation is a must. Start motivating yourself so that you can motivate others. Give your encouragement in a good way, so that neither of you will give up. Sports, after all, are a great way to communicate with each other.

APPRECIATE YOUR PARTNER FOR SOMETHING EVERY DAY

For each of us, it is very important to be appreciated by others, to be praised. This makes us feel good, gives us a positive self image, and makes us determined to do things better. And when that appreciation comes from a person we love, things are even better - praise coming from our life partner makes us feel like flying, like we are in heaven. Sometimes, a few words addressed to a loved one make true miracles happen for both partners. For the one who offers appreciation it is a good way to express what he or she feels, and for the receiver it is the perfect motivation to go further and to be a better person.

It often happens that you think nice things about your partner, but you fail to express them - you're too busy, or maybe you fear that he or she will become too proud. You have to remove all these obstacles and give yourself the chance to communicate your appreciation for the most important person in your life. You will see that if you do this every day, you will feel much closer to your partner, because your words of appreciation will make her or him feel loved and motivated to get even more appreciation from you.

You can start with simple things; for instance, you can praise your partner for the way he or she chooses to dress one day: "You look great today!", “I love the color combination of your clothes!” etc. If you’re not used to saying those kinds of words to your partner, give it a little try anyway. You will be amazed by his/her reaction. And you don't have to stop there - the next day you should say more words of appreciation. With time, you will learn to take advantage of every opportunity to praise your partner. If you do this exercise every day, you will get to discover great things about the one you love. In this way, you will come to appreciate him or her as much for the obvious aspects - the way he/she looks, dresses, speaks - as well as for the subtle details.

To appreciate the person you love is definitely a way to prove your love. When you appreciate your partner for something, he or she feels valued and wants to make things better and not to disappoint you. In turn, you will be appreciated in the same manner, and in this way, both of you will feel the joy of being appreciated by the other. There is nothing more pleasant to our ears than to hear some nice and sincere words coming from our partner. All we need to do is to feel free in expressing our positive opinions towards the one we love, and in this way we will grow closer to each other. Remember, little things mean a lot.

OFFER YOUR PARTNER HELP WHENEVER POSSIBLE – GREAT GIVERS ARE ALSO GREAT TAKERS

Generosity is a great quality in a person. Why shouldn't we use it in our relationships by offering help to our partner whenever we have the opportunity? Many times you feel like you have a lot of work, and you wouldn't mind getting a little help from someone. This means that your partner feels the same. If you offer your help, he or she will definitely appreciate the gesture and will be very grateful to you. To help the one you love with the daily chores or with any other work he/she has to do is another way of saying "I love you." Spontaneous gestures mean more than a thousand words.

There are people who are used to helping their life partners from the beginning of their relationship. This is a great thing, and it is worthy of all praise. But there are other people who need support to learn how to help their loved one. If you are among them, you need to know that it is not a hard thing to offer help to your partner. Here is how you can do it.

You can start by assisting with something that you know you can do successfully. For instance, if you are a man, you can you offer to wash the dishes for your wife, or, if you are a woman, you could do simple gardening work instead of your husband. Your partner will definitely be impressed with your help, especially if he or she isn’t used to such gestures from you. Of course, you don't have to limit yourself to a single occasion. You must be constantly mindful of the tasks that the other has to do, so you can offer your help. You might happen to come across things that you don’t know how to do. Don't worry; there's a solution for everything. You just need to have the necessary disposition to offer your help, and the rest will follow. For example, if you are a man, you can try to help your wife when she prepares meals, even if you don't know much about cooking. You can simply ask: "How can I help you?" Your wife will be absolutely enchanted with your proposal and will probably ask you to wash some vegetables, to slice the bread or do other simple things. But even if they are little, these gestures are very important to your loved one.

It is very nice of a person to offer help to anyone. Why would you think it would be bad to offer it to your spouse? Helping is a great proof of love. But I can tell you, it's not the helping that matters most but your presence when your partner needs a little help. You get to spend more time with him or her. You get to know your partner even better. At the same time, if you offer help constantly, you will see that your partner will offer you help as well. Of course, you don't have to think you will get nothing in return for the gestures that you make!

GIVE SMALL & INEXPENSIVE SURPRISE GIFTS ON A REGULAR BASIS

When it comes to gifts, everyone loves them. A gift may signify gratitude, appreciation and love from the one who offers it. Some people believe that the best gifts are the expensive ones because in this way they show they have stronger feelings. However, in couples' relationships, innovative and inexpensive gifts offered frequently could be a better option. The surprise felt when receiving a small gift from a loved one without any special occasion makes your heart beat faster every time. The small, nice gift speaks for the one who offers it and says: "I appreciate you more and more each day!"

It is regrettable that people used to give gifts only on special occasions. To surprise your partner in a pleasant way, you should follow this tip every day, or at least more often! You can even find original methods to offer your gifts! For example, you can send the gift to his office before he gets there. When he walks in and discovers the present on his desk, he will surely be moved by your gesture and will think of you all day long. You could just leave a gift on the bed in your room so that he or she will find it before bedtime, or maybe you wish to give it to your partner in the context of a romantic dinner. No matter how you choose to offer your gift, it will definitely have the same effect. It will produce joy in the one who receives it.

The value of the gift is not important; what really matters is its meaning. It is important to choose gifts that represent something. For instance, you can choose a cup with a love message on it, a personalized award certificate "For the most loving wife/husband!" or a picture frame with a photo of you two together. Of course, you can also opt for practical things such as a scarf, a pair of earrings or a postcard. Another important thing is to offer presents on a regular basis, for no special reason. You don't need any particular event in order to say "I love you!" using a small object that will always remind your partner of you. The effect will definitely be awesome every time – he or she will be excited by the idea of getting these small gifts and will feel much appreciated by you.

They say it is pleasant to receive a gift, but to give them is far better. If you make a habit of giving presents to your partner on a regular basis, you'll see this will have beneficial effects on you and the person you love. You will feel like teenagers who try to win one another's heart with a flower or a small but significant present. Make giving a habit. The value of the gift should not be given much attention, for a partner who appreciates your act of giving means the world. All you need to do is to put into that small object all the love that you feel!

LISTEN AND COMMUNICATE

When a fire in the fireplace is dying, we add coals to keep it burning. Who doesn't do this when it's cold? Like fires, relationships require a little effort to keep them going. It doesn't matter how you arrange the coals or where they come from; the only thing that matters is that you're not letting the fire die. It is a similar scenario with our relationships with our loved ones. We can't deny the fact that we may not be able to keep the flames hot and strong in a relationship for very long. What can you do to rekindle them if this happens to you?

Here is one way to reignite a relationship. You like to listen to your favorite music, right? You even sing along with it sometimes. This is because you feel a sort of connection to the music. There is something in it that stirs you and that keeps you listening to it and enjoying it every now and then. Now, let us compare that music with the "sound" of your relationship with your partner. Have you experienced the feeling of not wanting to listen to your partner anymore when you're having an argument? Or you don't even want to try to explain your side because you feel your partner doesn't listen to you? This really happens, and you are not the only person who has experienced it. Arguments can present a natural way of working things out, bridging the gap between the two of you and working through your differences. The problem is that you avoided the opportunity. You avoided a potential quality conversation.

I remember a video I've watched that says, "You make your problem, you make your solution, you make your results." Listen even if you think it's not worth it, and listen even more when it hurts. Whenever you feel like you don't want to listen anymore, give yourself a reason to do so. Forget about who's right or wrong; forget about your ego. Think of this: whenever children have problems with their playmates, they tend to fight. They say they will exclude a certain child from their group, and that they will not play with him again. But after several minutes, you will see them playing with him again. You will see them happy. You know why? It is because those children value their playmates more than their egos. I'm not telling you to go back to being childish, but if that is the only thing that can help you to appreciate the people in your life, then go back and play in the grass.

We are given ears so we can listen to others. But sometimes ears are not enough for us to truly hear. Why? Simply because when you are listening, you don't just have to hear the words; you have to understand them. Instead of your ears, use your heart to listen. We are given a mouth to speak, but sometimes there are better things to say than explanations and excuses. If you were the one listening, you would love to hear "sorry" rather than "because," right? You would be more pleased to hear "Can we talk about it?" than "Let's not talk about it." Isn't it so? This is why we need to listen with our heart and communicate, because love is always about understanding and not about proving anything.

INTIMACY / CELEBRATE LOVE WITH SEX

It is known that in a couple's relationship sex is very important. Making love is a great source of enjoyment for two people who have feelings for one another. It is the most profound form of communication between the two, a perfect way to show each other their love. Unfortunately, over time, a couple may face serious problems in terms of sex due to the development of a lack of interest. As interest fades away, the relationship slowly can become at stake, especially when distrust is involved or there is disappointment due to lies, misunderstandings, or an extramarital affair. But those who really want to keep their relationship burning need to know there are small changes that can keep their partner's sexual desire alive. Here are a few tips that can help you.

First of all, there are certain things you can do outside of your bedroom in order to awaken your partner's desires and fantasies. For example, when you are both at work, you should send him or her messages detailing sexy things that you would do if he or she were with you at the moment. This will make him or her impatient to get home and jump in bed with you.

Then, at home, before you go into the bedroom, you can surprise your partner with a romantic dinner with candles and soft music. If you are a woman, you may choose to dress in something sexy to stimulate your partner's visual senses. After dinner, foreplay has a significant role; why not start with a sensual massage with essential oils, which you can apply to your partner's body? If you want to make him or her feel everything more intensely, you may cover his or her eyes with a scarf. It's good for both of you to know each other's most erogenous zones, so that you will feel maximum pleasure. For a wonderful night of lovemaking, you need to emphasize that you just don't need your partner's body, but you want more than that his/her affection. Both of you should imagine yourselves at the center of the universe, loving each other deeply and wanting the other to feel good. You don't have to think about the way you look, whether you have done something wrong, or whether you're better or worse than former partners. You need to be active and involved! Talk with one another, and say what you like! As with other aspects of the relationship, communication is very important when you make love. Discuss things, praise each other, smile and feel good! Men are not very different from women in terms of enjoying praise. Their sexual confidence is based on what women say and on the way they feel.

To successfully create the best lovemaking, one should make note of two things: trust yourself, and you need courage. In order to maintain a solid relationship, it is very important to preserve the quality of the sex. That's why you must think constantly about how you can satisfy your partner better. You must keep in mind all the things that make him or her happy, including small details. To make the person next to you happy, you need to offer your whole self to him or her. You'll see how much you’ll be appreciated for what you do!

BE INVOLVED IN THINGS THAT YOUR PARTNER IS INVOLVED WITH

Understanding is one of the necessary things to keep the spark going in a relationship, and sadly to say, many men fail in this area. Because of pride, men, and even women, tend not to understand things about their partner. This can be because the partners live in different worlds, like strangers to each other. It is not easy for them to just accept things about each other, but they can if they are dedicated to doing it.

To some people, certain things their partners do seem strange or unreasonable. They can't understand why their partners are doing things that, to them, are not very important or they just don't want to do. There is a simple explanation: you and your partner have different priorities and interests, and although you are partners now, you should still have your *individuality*.

You started out so idealistic about your relationship. The truth is that you will always be who you are, and your partner will always be who he/she is. You will forever be different individuals, and your oneness will never be absolute. Live with it. If there are things she does that you don't like, she probably has the same kind of issue with you. The difference is that she may be doing something to understand you better, and so you should return the favor. The best thing to do is to be involved in some of the things that your partner is involved in. You might reply with astonished eyes and a big “WHAT?” Sorry, but you heard it right the first time. You have to learn to see the world the way your partner sees it in order for your relationship to work.

Why do we need to be involved in the things our partner is involved in? It comes back to the first word of this article: understanding. The purpose of this section is to help you understand your partner and learn how to show him/her your support. You can’t give your support with things you can’t accept, and you cannot accept things that you don’t understand, right? Of course, every rule has an exception. There are limitations on things you can be involved in. You can’t join your partner if she’s a member of an all-girl’s group, right? That’s a silly example, but what I’m trying to say is that you may join your partner in things you want to. If your partner loves collecting a certain kind of item, help your partner with the collection. Ask things about the item, and try to appreciate it. Try to understand what the items in the collection mean to your partner. Or, if your partner loves to cook, then cook with her. This will enable you to spend quality time together. Remember the word “try.” You can’t force yourself into those things, but you can always try.

As people grow, they change. The areas in which they change include their preferences, interests, desires, and more. As those changes take place, we must learn to understand some things. You and your partner might seem to live in totally different worlds, but being involved with each other's world can bridge the gap between you. This will enable you to grow and handle things in a more mature way. Loving is always good, and it'll get even better if you have understanding.

DON'T PLAY THE BLAME GAME; WORK THINGS OUT

Often, in a couple's relationship, the two partners tend to blame each in order to defend themselves. It is easier to put the blame on someone else than to be responsible and to recognize or admit your own mistakes. When something goes wrong in a relationship, people have a tendency to say: "It is your fault!" instead of recognizing their own flaws. The truth always lies in the middle: the two partners are both right and both wrong. The most correct way to solve things should be admitting to personal mistakes. To do this, we must first understand why we tend to lay the blame on others.

Psychologists say that we have a tendency to defend ourselves because of the sorrows that we have felt in the past, in our childhood and adolescence. To avoid suffering again, an individual has a tendency to defend himself and to throw all the blame on someone else. He believes that if he admits his own mistakes, he will be abandoned and this will make him suffer enormously. The key to a successful couple's relationship is to be aware of our limits and not to concentrate so much on our partner's flaws. To improve the relationship, you should be concerned constantly about changing something in your own behavior. Here are some ways you can do this.

First of all, you don't have to exaggerate things. For example, if your partner forgot to take out the garbage one day, you don't have to make a big deal out of it. Many times people tend very easily to notice the flaws of others and then hound them at every step, reproaching them if they didn't do things correctly. If you're going to start an argument accusing your partner of various things, he or she will probably retaliate in like manner, and it will be impossible to know whose fault it was. In such fights there is no winner. You have to keep your calm, analyze things, be willing to forgive other's mistakes and be open to communication. That does not mean you deny your problems, but put an end to the blame game and no longer accuse each other. Together, you must find a way of solving the problem you face. No matter how wrong of a thing your partner has done, you must show compassion and not make him/her feel even worse than he/she already feels.

It is always easier to put the blame on someone else in order to get out of a bad situation. But that is not a real solution for any problem. If you try to blame another person for what he didn't do well, he will always choose to defend himself and to accuse you of things that you've done wrong. In this situation you won't get anywhere. It is important to approach every situation calmly, to analyze information and to communicate with your partner in a constructive way.

LISTEN AS IF YOU HAVE NEVER TALKED BEFORE

If you want to win hearts, then cultivate the art of patient listening. Many of us are not aware that listening is a creative process through which we simultaneously give and receive love. We are instinctively drawn towards those who listen to us attentively. There is a magnetic attraction at work. The fact is that one who listens more learns more. Listen to your loved ones with rapt attention and interest, hanging on to every word they speak as if you have never talked with them before. Then sit back and watch the magic happen! It will work miracles for them and perhaps an even greater one for you. If you can train yourself at the task of listening rightly, you will solve most of your life's problems.

Nature gave us one tongue and two ears so that we could hear twice as much as we speak. Listening is a crucial art to master, and it stimulates better speaking. Get inside the heart and mind of the speaker. Listen with understanding. Maintain eye contact. Be non-judgmental and non-critical. Good listening reflects good manners and shows courtesy.

The speaker will feel appreciated, respected, comforted, understood and acknowledged. Listening creates acceptance, openness and builds strong relationships. A skilled listener listens to more than just the speaker's voice. He observes facial expressions and body language. Body language is equally as important as words. Your partner can see through your faked attention. Put yourself in their shoes when they talk. Do not interrupt to ask questions or change the topic.

Listening sharpens your awareness and wisdom. You will be introduced to a plethora of problems faced by others in society. The creative fountain in you will be stimulated, enabling you to meet your own life's challenges better. But do not get over-stimulated. Refrain from offering solutions to a talker's problem. Let the person do his own thinking and arrive at innovative solutions himself. People are happy when they know they have been heard. By listening, you are doing yourself a greater favor. It earns you respect and trust, enhances your relationship, cultivates a positive work environment, gains you greater repute and may earn you a friend for life. So take time to listen. All other things can wait.

Good listeners are very rare nowadays, and this could be the reason why they are treasured so much. Everybody wants to speak, and nobody wants to listen. To whom will you listen if not to your loved ones? Seek first to be a good listener and then to be understood. After all, to L.I.S.T.E.N. means to **L**ook interested, **I**nquire with involvement, be **S**ilent, have **T**rue empathy, **E**ncourage the speaker to open up, and take a **N**on-judgmental approach.

It is said that women are better listeners. Do not worry. Men too can master this elegant art with a little effort and practice. It is said, "The hands that serve are better than the words that preach." By listening, you are doing yourself and your loved ones the best service.

ALWAYS TREAT YOUR SIGNIFICANT OTHER AS IF YOU WILL NEVER SEE THEM AGAIN

Many couples have communication problems, and the two partners often quarrel. They say painful things to each other and do regrettable things like criticizing and offending each other. Their relationship becomes cold, and this often leads to separation. Building a strong relationship requires time and, more importantly, effort. Let us not get to the point where it is too late to fix things. You might be one of those people who end up saying: "*Why didn't I try to understand you better?*", "*Why I didn't give up fighting?*", or "*I should have been more understanding.*"

Such things happen every day around the world. An incident of conflict could happen to any of us and could separate us from the ones we love. Prevent events like this. Treat your partner well, keeping in mind that on any particular day you might not see him or her ever again. We can understand things better by relating to the experience of an old nun. The story goes like this:

The nun used to advise married couples to understand each other better. Once, a woman came to her and told her that she wanted to separate from her husband as he was treating her so badly. The nun asked her how she would feel if the man were to die soon. After a few years the woman came back and told the nun she had never split from her husband, thinking how sad she would feel if he were to die. Moreover, now they got along better with each other, and their life had become much better.

Each of us must learn from this story. In a relationship, the more you hold on to it, the more problems will come to test how strong it is. Remember that ugly words remain ugly and are always inappropriate. In the heat of conflict, you need to remember that the day you say ugly words to your partner might be last day you ever see him or her. You would surely regret what you said or did on that last day together. Instead of doing regrettable things, wouldn't it be better to prevent them? You need to realize that it is in your power to fix your communication problems. There is no other way or strategy to do this.

Life puts many obstacles in front of us, but it is too short for us to make it even worse with disagreements between us and our partner. There are always tense moments, but the aim is to treat each other with calm and patience. If only two people who live together would keep in mind the fact that the next day they could wake up single with no life partner, then surely they would exert more efforts to make things better in their relationship. If you realize that your partner deserves to be treasured and understood, then stay calm, be thoughtful and be more understanding. Not only so that fights will be avoided, but also to help the relationship work better. It's not hard! You can do this!

THINK BEFORE YOU SPEAK

Communication is very important in a couple's relationship. Sometimes they may use painful words instead of having a civilized discussion. Fights are often hard to avoid, and even the most successful couples have unhappy moments in their lives. Unhappy moments, however, should not always end up keeping you unhappy. You can communicate your sorrows or worries, which is important. That's why it is crucial for you to calm yourself before speaking. In this way you'll discover that you forget what made you so angry, or you'll come to the conclusion that your grief is unfounded. Eventually, you will be able to have a civilized and constructive dialogue.

Studies have shown that after an argument, it takes at least five positive events to neutralize the effects of that argument. It is always easier to prevent a fight than to repair a broken heart. You should learn to think before you speak. Here is how you can do this.

First of all, you must be more careful; you have to observe under what circumstances you said things that you regretted. Once you have figured out what kind of situations make you say hurtful things, you can exercise more caution whenever these occur. You can then try to understand better what your partner says. Issues often became clouded because things are not understood the way they should be. One person says something, the other interprets it as something else, and what do we expect to happen next? Of course: this is the point where fights begin.

Another important step in this process is to figure out exactly what you are thinking prior to saying it aloud. You should practice different ways of doing this. Finally, you need to choose the most suitable words to express what you feel, without offending the other person. You also have to anticipate your partner's reaction to your words. You have to think: *"What will he or she say if I say this?"* Make a habit of training your thoughts. Why? Because, often, the way we talk is a reflection of the way we think. If you raise your voice too much, do not expect to obtain positive results!

If you have had bad experiences and unpleasant fights with the person you live with, you must be aware that this is not just their fault but yours too. That's why you need to do all you can to make things better. You must learn to communicate your thoughts and feelings in a way that won't harm the other person. Thus, instead of saying: "*You are good for nothing*! *You're doing it all wrong*!" you can say, "*I can show you how to do this!*"

To demand that you develop qualities such as patience, calmness and understanding may seem to be asking too much. But these are special qualities that make a relationship great. Working on them is not hard, and wishing is not enough to make things better. It requires effort too!

LEARN FROM YOUR FIGHTS!

Life is not a bed of roses. It is a series of experiences, including some bad experiences. A wise person learns from them and uses them to his advantage. It is rather unfortunate that we too often fail to understand the power of a smile, a touch, or an honest compliment. A listening ear and the smallest acts of caring have inherent potential to turn a life around and strengthen human bonds. Though anger is a natural emotion, it is what we *do* while we are angry that endangers our health and our perception of others. It can cause irreparable damage to our relationships with our loved ones. Anger, moreover, is usually a cover up for other feelings like jealousy, an inferiority complex, insecurity or frustration. It is a way of blaming others for a situation.

While you cannot control your partner's anger, you can definitely control how you respond to it. If your priority is maintaining and strengthening the relationship rather than winning an argument, the highly volatile emotions will taper off quickly.

Be ready with positive, soothing words. Be focused. Always think in terms of the present to avoid bringing skeletons out of the closet. That will only add fuel to the fire. Conveniently forget all past grievances and maintain a positive attitude. Be respectful of your partner's opinion and live as his or her protective armor. To do this, you can start by reminding your partner of the best times you've spent together. Try to infuse good humor into every situation. Do not keep a solution to a problem to yourself; let your partner also see it.

Be caring and affectionate. Do not rebuke or be too critical, and do not neglect to deal with a problem till it blows up. Make it your principle to avoid emotional outbursts. Be prudent and analyze what triggers your partner's anger. It could be trivial issues like food, watching a favorite TV channel, not receiving your full attention (which usually happens when a baby arrives, depriving you of intimate moments), or even times when relatives are staying at your house.

It takes two people to keep an argument alive. When things are getting out of control, just disengage and walk away. Leave your partner alone for a while. Know when to let something go. If you cannot come to an agreement, then agree to disagree. Be the calm, positive force that makes him feel more accepted and happy. Be his emotional anchor. He needs you. Though he is an adult, he is still a child at heart.

DO SOMETHING TO PLEASE YOUR PARTNER IN THE EARLY MORNING

Life is the gift of God. Every single day of your life should be looked forward to and begun with cheer and optimism. Start the day with a smile and with a positive attitude. Every day is another chance at living a good life, and we should be grateful for that. Greet the sunshine, for this builds your inner strength to solve any problem that the day might bring as it unfolds. A day begun well is a day lived well.

To me “Life is a celebration.” I believe in living life to the fullest and savoring every moment of it. Starting the day doing what your partner likes the most is a gift a couple should share. Do it together. Frankly speaking, the best way to start a day is to start it with prayer. Holding each other's hand, calling upon the guidance of the Almighty is the most powerful guide to keep a relationship strong. Pray that you stay together, you eat together, live together and leave together; share truth immediately with each other and propagate the truth as you desire. Sharing the same viewpoint will slowly lead to a conversation about what you really want in life, without even putting forth effort to do it.

You can then follow the prayer by joining in your partner's morning routine. Say, for instance, your partner likes to walk the dog every morning; then accompany your partner and pooch on their stroll. Or maybe your partner enjoys having a cup of coffee on the back patio; then savor a cup of joe (or tea) along with him or her. Become a part of your partner's normal routine, which will show your partner a positive attitude and awareness of the things around you.

Mornings are always full of positive energy. Most mornings are spent planning and imagining what will happen during the rest of the day, so share, listen and take part of your partner's most relaxing and important moments. Don't be just a part of your partner's life; be part of your partner's plan.

It is a universal practice to start the day and to end the day with prayer. Children should be taught to pray at an early age. It thus becomes a habit. Prayer is an invaluable and invisible armor that keeps us connected. Generally we offer individual, silent prayers. They should be an expression of gratitude rather than begging for material comforts.

A moment shared together is a moment promoting positive developments in a relationship. Spending the first moments of the day with your loved one will make the relationship better from the very first time. A good first move may lead to a second good move. This has worked wonders for others. Try it - who knows what it can do for you.

"I" STATEMENTS FROM THE HEART

At the beginning of a couple's relationship, the two partners used to say loving words to each other on a regular basis. They felt like their hearts might leap out of their chests and they might explode if they didn't express what they felt. Unfortunately, over time, things change, and the partners begin to say more rarely the magic words: "I love you!" Some people never used to say these words at all. What we need to understand is the great power that statements from the heart have in a relationship and the importance of “I” in that statement.

It is difficult for those who are not used to saying the word “love.” It is even harder for them to include the word “I” along with it. If we have this difficulty of transforming our feelings into words, our relationship becomes at risk. Relationships are nurtured by acts of love, and this includes saying words of love and incorporating the personal word “I.” The first thing you have to do is to make sure that you correct your thoughts so that your actions are also corrected. You have to *show* that you care in order to be shown care in return. Rare are those who can love absolutely and never expect love back from their partner. Speak not only words of love but words that nurture warm feelings.

Before you go to work, for instance, kiss your partner and tell him “I love you!” He will definitely have a great day and will think of you the whole time. Or, if he happens to forget it, during the day, when you have time, you can send cute little messages like: *"I think today I made a big mistake: I forgot to tell you how much I love you!"* You shouldn’t be stingy with words; you have to think of how verbal expressions of love lead to better communication with your partner. Even if he doesn't really say the same things back to you, don’t be disappointed. After a while of hearing the magic words from you, he will learn to say them too. Of course, besides the classic "I love you!" there are many other ways for you to express your feelings. For example, you can tell your partner: *"I appreciate you enormously for what you do every day!"* or *"I find you very attractive!"* It is important that you keep the positive feedback coming and for your partner to hear more often that wonderful "I" coming from your heart. Stress and emphasize that word, for it is the only word that echoes you and your personality.

It is a pity that, over time, people forget to communicate their feelings to each other. It is a lot better to fill our mental scrapbooks with beautiful moments from the beginning of the relationship, back when we felt the need to say beautiful words to our partner every moment. Words have a magic power. With a simple "I love you!" you can give your loved one a fantastic day. All you need to do is open your heart and express what you feel! Don't think about whether or not you will receive words of love in return. To offer love, emphasizing that it is *you* who offer it, is simply wonderful!

AVOID YELLING AT EACH OTHER

Are you a rage-aholic? A rage-aholic is someone who is an "anger addict" and who gets excited by expressing anger. Would you like to be dubbed a "rage-aholic"? If your answer is no, then that is good news. What about living under the same roof with a rage-aholic? It is definitely a very bad proposition too. The good news is that you can avoid it by following certain tips that can actually save a marriage and thus create a happy home. Let us begin by understanding the concept.

Yelling is a poor behavior pattern. It is part and parcel of demonstrating anger. One yells or screams to relieve frustration. It is an attention-seeking behavioral pattern that gets aggravated when it is nurtured. A person is prone to yell and scream when he is extremely angry and with little or no provocation. Generally people who are chronically angry also compulsively express fits of anger.

When your partner is creating a scene at home with his anger and you want to play the role of peace keeper, then you must meticulously follow the following set of instructions. Never add to the screaming and yelling. It will just pour fuel on the fire. Mentally prepare with the following “must do”s and “must not do”s while confronting your angry partner. Understand that anger, which is the most complicated emotion, is displayed to establish dominance. So keep a cool attitude. First create the impression that you consider his flying into a rage to be immature behavior. Do not respond to his provocative words. Remain unfazed and take these tantrums in your stride. Never, ever give away through your words and body language the impression that you wish to retaliate. Be as calm as possible. You are, in fact, testing your own will power rather than your angry partner’s.

Doing these things will puzzle him, but still do not interrupt him. Interruption will guarantee more yelling and more slander. Do not stare at him. It will aggravate his already wounded ego. Do not change your facial expression. Rolling your eyes will be considered as mocking him and thus inflame him further. Do not criticize him. This is not the time for that. Do not bring up past incidents. Deal with the issue at hand. Do not threaten him with drastic repercussions for this showdown. It will increase his insecurity. Never make gestures like pointing a finger at him. This will make him feel small when he is now actually trying hard to appear larger and more intimidating. It will only make him yell and scream more loudly. Do not boast about yourself by flaunting your good qualities. He wants to feel like the hero by his angry outburst. Simply walk out of the room and appear busy with other work in order to try and dissipate the yelling.

Take responsibility to make the marriage work; this may include staying low as needed. Anger is a sign of weakness, but entertaining anger is worse. Love your partner and don't let him lose to his weakness. You are the winner even without straining your vocal cords, so bury the hatchet.

WRITE HIM A LOVE NOTE AND PUT IT SOMEWHERE LIKE IN HIS LUNCHBOX

We all love receiving love notes, but we can deny showing that we love receiving them to the extent that we will secretly read them over and over again but not talk about them. They fill our heart with tender feelings and are a personalized gift, the best way of expressing love. In today's world of fast technology, writing love notes is a forgotten art. They work wonders that regular text messages can never accomplish.

There is no hard and fast rule as to when you should write a love note and what it should contain. Let the situation decide. Sometimes we lose our temper, so use one to m*ake peace*. Sometimes out of annoyance we use harsh words and say the wrong things, leaving our partner feeling confused, hurt and angry.

Pacifying anger is a very difficult task. The best way out of this highly volatile situation is to write a love note, at which your loved one can't shout back. Don't make it too lengthy or sound like a sermon. It should take just a minute or two to read, but the message should linger on throughout the day till you and your partner meet again. Write how you really feel about a situation. Express your emotions freely. After writing such a note, you will breathe a sigh of relief, and then all the guilty feelings will just evaporate.

Writing a love note, moreover, does not only calm anger, it makes love true. Pay him a compliment on his sweet behavior, or say "You are my most valued possession." Express thanks when he helps you with daily chores, saving you precious time to deal with an important task, and write love notes more often when you want to correct shortcomings or misbehavior. Not only will your partner appreciate that you personally exerted the effort, but he will also understand the undeniable significance of the message itself, especially if he is surprised to receive a message in an unusual way. Put the love notes in such places where he will find them but will not expect them. It can be placed in his lunch box, in his socks, under his pillow, or in his locker. Be creative not only with your words but also with the way you deliver the note.

Love notes create a lasting memory of love or of mistakes that ended in love and forgiveness. They remain special treasures to everyone who receives them. Remember the time when you first got a love letter? Surely your partner will feel the same warm sensation when he is caught by surprise by your loving words. He will become more expressive, thoughtful and practice better life skills. Share and enjoy that invisible bond with your partner.

UNANNOUNCED VISITS AT THE OFFICE

When was the last time you surprised your loved one? How did you do it? Gifts are always good surprises, but there are other ways of pleasantly surprising your partner. One of those is an unannounced visit to your partner's office or place of employment.

Surprises are better if your partner can clearly see that you spent some time and effort on them. They don't need to be very elaborate, like a candlelight dinner with a glass of wine and a band playing in the background. It will take a lot of preparation for things like a night on board a cruise ship. A good surprise just requires you to put your heart into it and your willingness to make her feel very special.

How can a visit to your loved one's office be special? One condition is that you do it unpredictably. Do not let your partner have any idea that you are going to visit. You have to prepare and plan ahead. Why? Your surprise may go to waste if you do not have perfect timing. You will need knowledge of your partner's work schedule. Otherwise, there is a chance that when you make your surprise visit, your partner could be in the middle of a meeting. That would surely mess up the whole plan. Now, how can you prepare the right timing for your visit? If you don't know what your partner will be doing on the day you're planning your visit, you can ask her "indirectly." You may ask something like, "Dear, will you be available for a phone call tomorrow at 10 a.m.?" Of course your partner may wonder and ask why, so you have to think of a reason like "I want to call you then because I am planning to buy something special for dinner, and I may need help deciding what to buy, so I will probably call you from the store." Explanations like this should do the trick. If you can come up with a more creative story, then good; think of a better way of asking your partner "indirectly."

If you don't care to take the time to think up a good indirect question, or you don't want to have to stress out about the follow-up questions she may ask, then you can ask one of her co-workers, but please be careful with whom you choose. Choose someone who can keep your plan a secret. Once you have confirmed your partner's schedule, then it is time to think of a good "gimmick" for your visit. Yes, the visit itself will be surprising, but you'll want to do something that will tickle her even more. This is why you may need to bring flowers with you. Your attire should also be taken into consideration. You should aim to be the most handsome guy or the most exquisite lady in the room. Your partner will be so proud, plus he or she can then brag all around the office that he/she is very lucky to have you.

Gestures like this show that you care a lot about the relationship. If you can make your visit as pleasantly surprising as possible, then congratulations. This will surely show your partner how special she is to you, and even during those times when she is feeling very busy or overwhelmed, she will be reminded that there is someone who can help lighten her load.

SEE THINGS FROM YOUR PARTNER'S PERSPECTIVE

We all desire an ideal marital relationship, but we may know our marriage is not faring as well as we expected. The reasons are diverse, but the most conspicuous reason for failure in relationships is the inability to see things from your partner's perspective. You have failed to gather sufficient knowledge of your partner's interests, passions, mood swings, pleasures and pains, cravings, positive traits, value system and most significantly his perspective on life. This means you have failed to do your necessary homework as a partner. Your partner thus remains a stranger to you even after years of wedded life. The more deeply you come to know him, the greater the compatibility will become between you both.

Don't have unrealistic expectations. Your partner is unlikely to fit into your mental mold of an ideal partner. So, take a positive view and acknowledge your partner's positive traits with admiration and fondness. Respect change, as change is inevitable. Show maturity by appreciating and valuing these changes.

The best way to see things from your partner's perspective is to listen and not block out truth. Turn toward and not away from your partner. To see things the way your partner does, to think the way your partner thinks, and to understand the way your partner understands, you must create a connection that will wire your life to your partner's. To achieve this, first create a joint emotional account. Be ever ready to support your partner's hopes and dreams. Be familiar with and show interest in your partner's world. Strong, long-lasting marriages are the ones in which power is shared. Ask about his work at the office, his colleagues, his friends and hobbies. There should no longer be talk of "your family" and "my family." It is now "our family."

The moment you do create this emotional bank account, you can connect to your partner more strongly than ever before. Be aware that marriage is not merely making love, raising kids, sharing chores and partying together. It is about being more receptive, adaptive and accommodating to your partner's views, perspective, opinions, culture and lifestyle, thus ensuring an overall pleasant ambiance in your home. `

Emotionally wise couples are familiar with each other's goals, worries and hopes. Marriage that involves love, romance, friendship, emotions and shared responsibility is worth working at with full zeal and fervor. Be more affectionate, attentive, supportive and humorous towards your partner. The more love, respect and honor you bestow on your partner, the more of those same things you will receive. Be flexible and never take a stubborn stance.

Participate in activities that keep you emotionally connected like attending parent-teacher conferences together at your kids' school, or taking family vacations.

ASK YOUR PARTNER WHAT YOU CAN DO FOR HER TODAY AND DO IT

When it comes to the responsibilities in a couple's relationship, it is a marvelous thing for the two partners to share them, so that neither of them should feel at a disadvantage. Many misunderstandings between partners happen because one of the partners has too many things to do, and the other doesn't notice this or never offers to help. It would be wonderful if your partner asked you what he could do for you and then worked hard to accomplish that task. If this would prove the case, why shouldn't you ask your partner for help? Surely the person you love most will be more than happy to accept your help too, and this will bring you closer to each other.

Usually, in couples' relationships, women are the ones who take on most of the responsibilities. A woman cooks, cleans, goes shopping, and carries and raises children. Often, a woman has to do a lot of things on her own, and this depletes her energy and can cause dissatisfaction. She may start to pass blame on her husband. This situation can be prevented if the man is more aware of his wife's daily activities. He might give her a call and simply ask: "Is there anything I can do for you today?" He will probably get an answer like: "Yes, I would like you you to pick this up from the store," or "You can pay the bills," or "It would be great if you got the kids after school." These are not things you can't do. These are common activities that your wife performs frequently, but you can do them just as easily. By helping her in this manner, you will obtain two great things: you will understand your wife better, and she will appreciate you more.

On the other hand, women should also ask their spouses what they want and do the same. Your husband may say, "I want to have hot sex tonight." So do it. You should be thankful that your husband asks for it instead of demanding it from you. Or maybe all he wants is to spend the night out eating lobster in a restaurant; then go. Plan an evening on which to do what he has been longing to do. It is good to submit to your partner's requests once in a while.

With this activity, it doesn't matter what the answer might be to your question. What is important is that you ask the question. Asking shows your partner he or she is important to you. The fulfilling of your partner's want or need is the bonus factor.

You may think of asking what your partner wants but fail to actually ask. What good does just thinking bring you? None, in this area. It doesn't let your other half know that you care about his/her needs. That's why it's good for you to inquire about what he or she wants. Your partner will appreciate you twice: first because you were concerned about him or her, and second because you did what you were asked.

SURPRISE, SURPRISE

Each couple's relationship needs something spectacular, something unpredictable to make the monotony disappear. Simply telling someone "I love you" every day can turn into a habit that loses any charm or meaning after a while. To keep the magic alive in a relationship, it is better to perform a few small but impactful gestures, as this is known to have enormous value. It will make your partner feel special and treasured. You can change a boring, routine relationship into an award-winning love story by doing a few simple things to pleasantly surprise the person you love. Thus, not only will you reduce the distance that has been created between you, but also your partner will be extremely happy with the surprises you offer and will certainly reward you. Here are some effective ways that will help you to impress your partner and prove the intensity of your feelings.

First, I want to break up the concept of "surprises" into categories, for surprises can be given in many ways. In this activity, you are encouraged to try two different kinds of surprises. They are surprises with material gifts and surprises in the realm of feelings.

With the first kind of surprise, you must choose a gift that will show you are an inventive person. You can offer your partner a gift certificate to a Thai massage parlor, a personalized pillow with your photo on it or a T-shirt with a message of love from you. If you are a woman, you can give your boyfriend or husband tickets to a football game, and if you are a man, you can surprise the one you love by taking her on a trip to a quiet, relaxing place.

With the second kind of surprise, you have to catch your partner in a situation where he or she will not be expecting you to do the kind of thing you are about to do. This involves trying new things. Say, for instance, smelling your partner after every shower. This is kind of silly, but it is sweet. You can also give your partner a surprise kiss at times when he or she is deep in thought. Your partner will definitely stop thinking about whatever it was and will think of cuddling you instead.

Perform the surprise without any specific reason. Don't worry; there are plenty of ways you can catch your partner in an unexpected situation. Practice this often but not in the same way. It is important to maintain the element of surprise in this activity. Just make sure that your surprises are pleasant. Everyone loves pleasant surprises, and when they come from the one we love, they are doubly alluring. A surprise banishes the monotony of your relationship, so try them out and have fun.

TREAT YOUR PARTNER AS YOUR EQUAL

We all wish to have a healthy relationship with our spouse. A healthy, thriving relationship requires some "give and take." Mutual respect and love form the basis for a strong relationship. Never adopt a superior and dominating attitude towards your partner. Do not look down on his deficiencies and shortcomings. Help him to overcome those flaws and build up his positive traits. Nobody is perfect. Are you?

Are you just married or happily married? A truly successful marriage is one between equals. You can transform your marriage's status by changing your attitude towards your partner. Review your expectations. Accept your partner as he is. Ponder his winning qualities and learn to forgive when he commits mistakes. Never criticize, condemn or censure. Be realistic. Try putting yourself in his shoes and viewing the situation from his angle. You will understand that you have been making his life miserable if you're constantly nagging and using sarcasm. Will there be love in such a relationship? For love to blossom, make consistent efforts to mend the relationship before it is too late.

Listen to your partner sympathetically. It will enable you to resolve conflicts without arguing. It is an opportunity to explore each other's personalities more fully. Begin by showing your affection for him. These are the small pleasures in life that you should cherish and never miss, for they silently and effectively strengthen the bond between you. Then follow that by giving positive feedback on things about him to others. Praise his achievements and virtues before your relatives and friends. Tell the world how helpful he is and how you cannot manage without him. This way your partner will know that the things he does also matter in the marriage.

The next step is not to compete with your partner's achievements. Your achievements, though different, are equally as important as his/hers are. Make it a point that you are equal to your partner in authority and in accomplishments. You have to communicate wisely with your partner. Full honesty, however, is not always wise. Learn to ignore shortcomings to boost your partner's feelings. Bad communication causes most broken marriages. The way you say things is more important than what you say.

Behind every successful marriage there is a wise partner who knows the value of love, respect and honor. So work with the spirit of a scientist and the soul of a romantic to ensure a harmonious and long-lasting relationship with your partner. Treat your partner as your complete equal.

NEVER HANG ONTO UNWANTED BAGGAGE

Carrying over unresolved baggage from the past leads to bitterness in a marriage. Our upbringing and our experiences during our childhood years greatly influence our thought patterns, notions and values. People tend to re-live these past events in their adult years. If you wish to improve the quality of your marriage, then stop hanging onto unwanted baggage. Do you want a happy life or one filled with anger, resentment, frustration and suspicion, which suck out happiness and excitement from the relationship?

Life presents us with several challenges. Whether you think you can or think you cannot – you are right. Propagate the right mindset. Try developing the following skills.

Take the first step by moving from seeing things as problems to viewing them as possibilities. Are you prejudiced toward a certain way of handling money or bringing up your children? Focus steadily on what you can control, leaving alone what you cannot. You must understand that there is always a way out. So, develop a clear picture of your desired outcomes.

Ask purposeful questions of yourself and your partner. Inquire about what your partner desires and needs from you. Be a willing emotional anchor. Overcome negative emotions, which eat you away by spreading unpleasantness. The best way is to focus on the situation at hand and try not to connect events in the past to what is happening now. You only aggravate a situation by attaching too much importance to it.

So draw inspiration from your circle of friends and relatives. Identify those couples who have happy and successful relationships. Emulate them. If possible, seek friendly advice. Follow their wise counsel and you will benefit a lot from others' experiences with similar emotions and situations. This will help you to tackle yours better. Talk openly about issues you are bitter about. Love unconditionally. Divulge your hidden thoughts and feelings. It is the only way to get rid of baggage you are not supposed to carry.

Unwanted baggage is just a burden on your relationship. Identify a negative emotion that has seized you and express it without restraint. When you acknowledge and honor each other's feelings, you feel better. All the built-up pressure is vented out.

Thus, by leaving unwanted baggage behind, we move forward no longer harassed by negativity, which impedes togetherness physically, mentally and morally. Give up your victim mentality and go for healthy alternatives. There should be some give and take. This will help you find peace within. It is worth trying. Just as you take out the trash at your house to keep it tidy, in the same way we should never hang on to unwanted baggage in our relationships.

TALK, SHARE, DO NOT ARGUE ABOUT FINANCIAL RESOURCES

Financial prudence lies at the heart of a thriving marriage alliance. Though it is very easy to enter into a marriage, keeping it intact is a herculean task. Financial problems can spoil marital bliss. Even couples who seem to agree on everything else may disagree on financial matters. This disrupts the otherwise tranquil atmosphere. Though money is a sensitive issue, do not feel awkward about discussing it. It is better to talk and share openly rather than to argue over financial issues. Work out a suitable financial strategy; otherwise, you could be caught in financial straits that will choke the life out of your marriage.

Mapping out your finances is essential. This will give you a clear picture of your financial status. Lack of money, lack of control on spending and lack of fallback savings lead to financial showdowns that can cause fissures in relationships. Good communication is the key to all marital and financial challenges. If you want a friction-free marriage, then put your finances in order. Though it is not romantic, it is the most important task to attend to.

The first thing you have to do is to prepare a written monthly budget on earnings, savings, spending, investments and borrowing. It should be realistic and reasonable, and you should resolve to stay within its boundaries. Write down clearly how much money you earn. Do you have debt? If yes, how much? How much income do you expect to earn in the future? Will it be able to cover your growing expenditures? If you expect it to drop, then how will you manage it? Will you be able to maintain your current lifestyle with your spending habits? Do you have a sufficient retirement fund? What are your plans for helping the kids, such as putting them through college? How much liquid cash do you wish to have on hand?

The second step is to allow a fair margin for rising inflation levels. Keep aside a discretionary amount of funds for this purpose. You should also decide who will manage the funds. The partner who has better money skills can take charge of the difficult task of keeping track of your monetary inflow and outflow. This will reduce financial stress, and you will have a clearer picture of your assets and liabilities.

The third step is to review your budget periodically. Ideally, this review should be done on the last day of each month. Negotiate and re-negotiate to make necessary amendments to your financial profile if required. If you talk and share openly, it will greatly help avoid arguments.

Marriage is a joint venture in which both partners should play an active role in financial planning. Disagreements on financial matters trigger marital conflicts. Eliminate impulsive buying habits and only make planned purchases. Never spend money you do not have. Do not fall into the traps of zero rate finance or easy EMIs to purchase durables, as these add to your debt burden. Be prudent while using credit cards. Having the entire family use a single credit card is a good idea. Only then can you allot sufficient funds towards investment. Never use money as a weapon against your partner. Talking and sharing ensures financial discipline and indicates good house-keeping. Strong money skills pave the way to stronger marriages. Financial therapy involving talking and sharing solves most marital disputes.

DISPLAY AFFECTION WHENEVER YOU CAN, EVEN IN SIMPLE WAYS

A good relationship is built on comfortability with one another. A comfortable couple doesn't usually feel the need to constantly show affection. Most observers would agree that less is more when it comes to a couple's public displays of affection. The truth in relationships, as in life, is that it doesn't matter what others think. If two people decide they would like to show a little or a lot of affection in public, this is their own decision. When it comes to affection, the question isn't "when" but "how." In this activity, you'll learn the answer to this question through a variety of different techniques. Now, let's uncover how to use them to add some spice, plus something nice, to your relationship.

Step 1: Holding hands. The Beatles had it right when they wrote their hit song "I Want to Hold Your Hand." Holding hands may seem like the most insignificant of ways to show affection, but it truly can mean a lot to your partner. Whether you lock hands for a second or for a long time, you'll find the effort really makes a difference. Holding hands is about affirmation. It means you care about a person beyond your libido. You'll find that these simple and sweet ways to show affection are among the most meaningful things in a relationship.

Step 2: Hugs. Along these lines, hugs are also some of the best ways to show your partner that you truly care. We often greet our partners with a hug and kiss, but beyond that we can forget about the power of a hug. It is scientifically proven that a 15-second hug can improve your day, so try giving your partner a long hug every once in a while. Or, grab a hug in the brief moments before you head off to work or a dinner party. Remember, simple and conservative ways of showing affection can serve as a great reminder of just how much you care for your partner.

Step 3: Kisses. A kiss may be the most intimate form of affection we allow others to see. Couples can easily forget the power of a peck. Sure, making out is very nice, but when you are busy and in public this may not be the best option. A few pecks quickly shared between two people who understand each other can do the trick. If you and your partner can learn to begin exchanging more kisses throughout the day, you'll find that both of you will be happier with one another.

These little tricks are nothing special. They are just some simple ways to continue to show affection throughout your day. The basics can be the most important parts of a relationship. Look at the relationships you've seen around you that are thriving. There are no fancy tricks to having a great one. No, a good relationship is built on the desire to be with your partner. A healthy amount of affection is an important part of this. The idea isn't to try too hard to prove to your significant other that you care for him or her. Instead, the idea is just to care for him/her in the most natural and casual ways you can. Hold your partner's hand in the car. Hug your partner when he isn't expecting it. Kiss her every time you have a chance. Take all these types of affection and make them a part of your everyday life. Every relationship is different; lots of variety exists from couple to couple. Still, everyone should understand that the small things you do for each other are going to be the most important ones in maintaining a flourishing relationship.

BE SUBMISSIVE TO EACH OTHER

We are never wrong. Or at least we would prefer to think so. We often think of arguments in our relationship as battles. In this analogy, the two people in a relationship are warring countries at each other's throats. Doesn't sound very pleasant, does it? Considering that you are both choosing to share at least part of your life together, it may be best to change your way of thinking. The truth is that we are wrong a lot. Knowing this can help change the way we look at our relationships. What if, instead of arguments, we were just having a conversation? Instead of trying to win, we were trying to understand? Changing the way we interact with our partners isn't that difficult. This change is based on a simple, three-step process: listen, counter, and (if needed) compromise.

Many arguments are based on misunderstandings. Simply listening to what the other side has to say can end an argument. People can sometimes feel as though they aren't being heard, and this can cause them to lash out. Showing that you care and are willing to listen your partner can end an argument, or at least help ease the situation. Listening can be difficult, though, especially when two people are already angry with each other. When trying to be a good listener, do not interrupt, listen actively and show empathy. Active listening can sometimes be the most difficult of these because it can come across as facetious relatively easily. Try your best to be sincere at all times; this will help your partner remain calm as you begin to explain the way you feel.

Countering can be difficult because it requires you to express how you feel without being rude. The first rule is to not ridicule your partner's position. You may want to explain why they are wrong and you are right, but there really is no point to that, since people stop listening when their views are being attacked. Instead, tell your side of the story; focus on what you see and feel. The point is to create some understanding of what you are trying to tell your partner and why. After you both have spoken, you should both understand how the argument began.

Knowing why an argument began is different than ending it. The next step is, of course, trying to figure out how to avoid this argument in the future and apologize to each other. Compromising is what usually needs to happen in order to prevent further conflict. We all know this is more easily said than done. However, where there is a healthy amount of compromise, there is a healthy relationship. Never compromise more than you feel you should, though. Eventually you would grow tired of finding yourself changing too much for your partner.

We all want to win. Arguments, especially in relationships, are not competitions. Instead, they are moments when you can learn the most about your partner. Think of arguments as conversations involving differing opinions. Although this definition may overlook the obvious heated language, it helps us realize the virtue of an argument. Remember: compromising isn't losing; in fact, it is closer to winning. The difference is how you view the "teams" involved in an argument. The opposing sides, as they should be, consist of you and your partner against whatever conflict is causing you to fight.

CREATIVE AND SPECIAL GIFTS

Think about your partner. Think about his laugh or, better yet, what makes him laugh. Think about all the little oddities that work together to make him unique. Consider all this and then try to imagine what your partner really would like to receive as a gift. You may not be able to guess exactly what he would want, but that isn't the point of giving a gift. A gift is every bit as much about you as it is about him. Of course, we have all stared at a newly unwrapped gift, pondering "How do I fake liking this one?" but that doesn't mean we don't want to receive a surprise gift now and then. In fact, the best gifts often are the ones we're not expecting. The line between unexpected and unwanted can be very thin, though. Mastering the tightrope of taste is never easy. However, you may be able to create a safety net if you follow these guidelines: be creative, unique, and unpredictable.

Not everybody thinks he is creative, but if we all thought this about ourselves then we would be wrong. The real problem is that not everyone's creativity has been nurtured. If this is the case for you, or even if it isn't, let yourself discover how to choose a creative gift. The journey begins with your thought process. Hopefully, you are already thinking about what makes your partner special; now think about what can help bring out these distinguishing qualities. Maybe your special someone has the most amazing blue eyes and you want to help her show off that feature. Look for something she would wear in a shade that brings out those baby blues.

Choosing something your partner is bound to like but never would buy himself is a great way of being unique. You want the gift to have that stamp on it that reminds him of you. If it is a major holiday or birthday, he is going to be getting all types of gifts, so make sure that yours is different than everyone else's. Unique shouldn't mean bizarre, unless that reflects your personality; it should show your individuality. A shocking gift isn't the key to a great gift; personality is. A mug is just a mug. But a mug from a town you two first visited together is a fond memory.

After you've decided on a gift that is both creative and unique, your gift really will be unpredictable. When you are trying to be unpredictable with your gift, it's all about choosing the right time to reveal it. If it is for a birthday or holiday, give it right before everybody else gives theirs. In the car before you take off to the party, set the gift on her lap. Or, the night before her birthday, cook her a special, delicious dinner. Remember that an unexpected gift is always welcome, so buy her a gift "just because."

Coming up with the right gift really can be an art - a process of trying to approach a concept in your own way. As with any art, you'll want to be creative, unique and unpredictable. You won't get exactly what your partner might expect, but you'll find they will love your gift just the same. As long as you stick to these guidelines, you can't go wrong. Don't be afraid to spend quite a while thinking about what gift you'll get. Remember, it's the thought that counts; if you think for a long time with these guidelines in mind, you are bound to find the right gift.

CUDDLE ME UNDER THE STARS

Being in a long-term relationship may result in two different things: lots of love or lots of trouble. Maintaining a balance between sentimental issues and daily life can be tricky when routine interferes. Routine can tear apart even the loveliest couples, but the good news is that there are ways of keeping the passion flowing. Scientists have demonstrated that the chemicals involved with falling in love change after a certain period; the endorphins, which create more euphoria, eventually give way to oxytocin, which produces a feeling that is more related to commitment and stability. Nevertheless, it's possible to reawaken the euphoric flames; some simple tips can help you escape from ordinary life and bring your partner along.

Many couples arrive at a phase where they will use just about any excuse to fight, in order to make up afterward. This may result in an unhealthy relationship, and it may not work so well.

First, step outside your comfort zone, forget about watching movies, turn off your TV and practice more interpersonal communication. Ask about each other's day, beyond what you would normally ask. Then get ready to go outside, but forget about the mall or about visiting friends; set some time aside exclusively for the two of you to spend alone together. A good way of keeping the passion flowing is to try activities you wouldn't normally do: go hiking during the weekend, take Monday off and enjoy a Sunday sunset, then cuddle under the stars. You can walk along the beach, lie together in the sand or sit down in the middle of a bridge on top of a freeway and wait for night to arrive. As it gets colder, holding each other under the stars will inspire romantic feelings.

Feel the calm night, the cool air, the twinkling of the stars, listen to each other's heartbeat, and touch each other. You don't even have to say a word. Just enjoy this adventure under the sky. You can play a game like kissing without touching each other. Remember why you've chosen your partner; be thankful for what he or she offers and the fact that you're not wandering alone. Being grateful and showing your partner how much you value his or her company is a fast way to feeling the way you felt on your first date.

As with almost everything in life, relationships work in cycles; you may not always be burning for each other, but you will be able to revive the flames from time to time. The outdoors is a great place to remind each other of why you're together; there are no distractions, and there's a lot of space for the two of you to forget about everything else. Remembering why you're together will help you be grateful for each other, being grateful for each other will revive the flames, and being out under the stars is the perfect space to encourage all the love that's happening.

EXPERIMENTING IN THE BEDROOM

After reading this title, you may have trouble not giggling. Why is that? Everybody knows what this means and is a little curious, but many people don't take it seriously. In a relationship, experimenting with your sex life can help cure ailments such as boredom, routineness and - worst of all - loss of passion. So, maybe, stop giggling and keep reading? In this article, you'll learn some of the milder things you can add to your sex life to make things a little more interesting. We'll start with the very famous Kama Sutra, move on to talking dirty, and finish with opening a dialogue with your partner about some other things you may be interested in trying.

No doubt you have heard of the Kama Sutra, but this book isn't exactly what you think. The Kama Sutra isn't just a list of different types of positions, and I'm not selling it either. What I'm trying to say is that the book actually has a lot more to it; it includes some great tips on life and love as well. There are all sorts of things in it that will change your view of sex. So, start reading books like this - not just the Kama Sutra, although it's nice to begin with.

Talking dirty may come naturally to you or may not come at all. It is very subjective what is *dirty;* with different people it can vary from a few swear words to a few acts that are still banned in more conservative places. So, really, when you are beginning, less is more. The last thing you want to do is turn each other off. Done correctly, though, dirty talk can make sex feel completely new and full of adventure. The act of simply whispering not-so-sweet nothings in your partner's ear can add a whole new dimension to your relationship. More importantly, it can make you feel more sexual and open to discussing new things that you may have been too coy or shy to speak about before. Talking dirty can create a new element of danger in your sex life and open dialogue about other things to try. Remember, anything that you would like to try in bed is best talked about, at least a little bit. Don't discuss each topic to death, but make sure both parties are interested and willing.

There is so much more that you can do with your partner in bed. There are all sorts of videos and toys that are designed to help you experiment with your partner. Discussing this type of thing with your partner can be tough, though. Mention something that you might want to try and then carefully evaluate his or her reaction. Considering that you two are in a relationship, odds are that you may be interested in doing similar things in bed. However, being too blunt or overzealous may cause your partner to feel uncomfortable with an idea. Ask and then give it time. Any time you try something new in bed with your partner and he or she really isn't into it, the sex just isn't as much fun. Be empathetic.

TIME TO MAKE TIME: BUSY COUPLES SHOULD SCHEDULE SEX

Ever find yourself arguing with your partner for no apparent reason? You could be at each other's throats about something as trivial as doing the dishes, and neither of you will let up. Busy couples may find themselves fighting with each other more often. There are a variety of reasons why this may be happening, but among the most common is one of the easiest to fix: a lack of sex. Yes, not having sex regularly enough can turn two people in love into a pair of very angry people. You may chuckle at this, but it is true.

The best solution for busy couples is as easy as making the time. Make up a schedule. Maybe this method doesn't sound very romantic, but in this you'll learn to make time and still hold onto the passion of it all. The steps are easy: first, choose a day. Then, make that day special and unique. Third, woo your partner and turn back into the very in-love people you once were.

Any day will do. Any time will do. Just find a day you'll both be able to be present physically and emotionally.

Everybody is busy, but there are bound to be a few hours in the week that you can devote to your relationship. Maybe the time and the day will need to change weekly, but the important thing is that it happens. Start by talking with your partner, asking to set aside a little time in both of your schedules for your relationship. Remember, sex isn't just always about orgasm or physical pleasure. Instead, it can be an affirmation of your mutual love. So, don't just ask to have more sex, be tactful. Focus on making the experience something new and not just another time.

Once the time is set aside, try to be creative with each date. Try to think about the things that will get you and your partner in the mood. Be romantic. Even if you only have fifteen minutes between showering and going to work, wear the perfume/cologne that will make your partner swoon. It doesn't matter what you do, just that you cater to your partner's desires. Getting yourselves in the mood is what this step is all about. You need to make the most of every moment you have with your partner, because you aren't always going to have this opportunity. You'll find that working in such a finite amount of time will add to the passion of the moment.

Wooing someone is something that is usually a part of the dating process. Once we've been with our partner for a long time, we can forget this part of sex. Wooing starts with step two, but it should continue on to sex. Change up the routine a little bit. Focus on your partner's needs for a little longer than usual. The best part of these dates is that they will help rejuvenate the passion that has been lacking lately. You'll find that the more you give, the more you'll receive. So, don't be afraid to be sexy for your partner.

Making your schedule fit your sex life is completely up to you and is the only the first step. Be sure to "wow" your partner by making every date memorable. Continue those unforgettable moments into sex; make every moment special by doting on his or her needs. Once you've started following these steps in your life, you'll begin to realize you aren't at your partner's throat quite as often. The easy way not to make a change in your relationship is saying you just don't have time; make the time. You'll see you'll be waiting for that day to come.

KEEP YOURSELF PHYSICALLY FIT

Have you heard all the jokes about couples getting fat together? Yes, there are a lot of those. They can be discouraging for all sorts of couples, but there is such a thing as being in a committed relationship with both your partner and with fitness. How it's done, though, takes some compromise in your life and with your partner. There is nothing wrong with gaining a little weight when you have been with someone for a long time. People who are no longer insecure about trying to find that special someone no longer kill themselves to stay fit. Nobody says you need to look like you did at 22 for the rest of your life, but if you are interested in some ways to stay healthy and grow with your partner, then this article is for you. We'll cover some ways to avoiding falling into the habits that cause couples to gain some extra love handles. We'll also briefly talk about healthy eating and great activities that help burn calories.

Those who are thoroughly enamored with one another have a hard time leaving the bedroom. Sex actually is a great way to burn calories, so this isn't all bad; however, this type of behavior encourages a bad behavior as well. So, what are these behaviors, and how do you avoid them? Well, when you are tired after a romp in the sack, you may be more likely to eat poorly; avoid fatty foods and sugar, like fast food and ice cream. Sex does burn calories, but not enough to justify spending all day in bed. Take a break in between kisses to go on a walk. Just try to avoid being lazy and eating too much while falling for one another. Once you have already established these habits, it will be difficult to break them.

Eating healthily is one of the best ways to fight off those extra pounds. Making dinner at home can be a fun activity as well. Making food at home allows you to take control of the type of foods that you will be eating. Lean meats and colorful veggies are two really great foods that are both healthy and delicious. Keeping to these types of meals, whether you are at home or out, will definitely help you and your partner drop some of the extra pounds you have accumulated. Do not, however, get involved with fad diets and cleanses. Just stick to clean eating.

Working out, moreover, doesn't have to be done in the gym on a treadmill; playing the sports you enjoy can be a great way to stay fit. Why not start by teaching your partner about the sports that you love? This will also help strengthen your relationship. So tell your partner about your college tennis days or kick around a soccer ball. If you never were into sports, try walking and then eventually running together; both are conducive to conversation and burn a lot of calories. It doesn't matter what you'll be doing; just spend at least 45 minutes doing it every day.

A couple that stays fit together stays together. Sure, you'll both look good and that's always a plus, but you'll both be healthier and you'll have bonded over the struggle. Stay away from falling into the stereotypes that come with being in a committed relationship. Stay fit by just eating right and working out. Put your single friends to shame and make them regret ever making a joke about letting it all go.

KISS ME BEFORE YOU LEAVE

Kissing is one of the sweetest moves for partners. The moment your lips touch hers, a million sensations are released and electrify your whole body. Indeed, no couples should miss out on this. Busy schedules at work or any other things shouldn't hamper partners in spending a moment for a kiss.

Do you kiss your partner before you leave your house? If you do, then that is good for you; if you don't, you must start doing it as a habit now. Do you know why? It is because it's a big thing for your partner. A simple kiss can convey infinite meaning and feeling. It reminds her that wherever you will go during that long day, whatever you will do and whoever you will be with, you will end that day by coming back to her. It's like saying "I will just go to work" (if you're going to work) and nothing more. It is like assuring her through reminding her that you live your life for her.

A very simple kiss has very complex meaning. This step seems easy, right? You may think that you just have to kiss her whenever you're going out and that's it. If you think that way, then you are wrong. The purpose of this article is to add or reignite the sparks. You don't give a kiss as a requirement; you do it as a habit.

What is the difference? If you do it as a requirement and what you are thinking is that you "have" to kiss your partner before you leave, then your kiss will be like a voice whispering in her ears: "He is just doing it because he has to." So do you think that will be fine with her? Of course not. But if you're doing it as a habit, your kiss will say to your partner "He's kissing you because he wants to." "Has" and "wants" definitely have different meanings. We do not need to talk about how you'll do it, because kissing is very simple, but the feeling and intention it carries matter the most.

Kissing your partner before leaving will be better if you add sugar coated words like, "I'll be back early tonight for dinner, and I'd love to have your (a dish she cooks well)."

And always wear a smile when leaving. You can look back to show her that you're happy to have her as your partner. Leave her feeling inspired to cook well for you. This will ease all the boredom that she would have endured in her long day without you.

Your kiss is like saying "I'll be home for you soon." This will bring her excitement. Give her something to look forward to at the end of the day. After long hours of not being together, it will be good if you give her another kiss when you come back home. Make her feel that you missed her as badly as if you'd been apart for a long time. Lastly, before ending your day, giving your partner a kiss in bed will be perfect before you drift off to dreamland.

DON'T DEMAND THINGS FROM YOUR LOVE ONES, REQUEST

Loving is about giving. This might be a cliché you often hear. Though this is true, we can't deny the fact that as human we, sometimes, want something from our partners. Some of us waits until our partners provide us that something, some requests for that something, some asks, some demands. This doesn't apply only on material things. Sometimes we want a certain attitude of our love one to be changed. Often times, things like this become a source of misunderstanding.

Whenever we want something from our love one, whatever it is, we must remember not to demand it, we must request for it. When a demand is made by someone it implicates authority over someone being demanded. Do we want our partners to feel that authority. It is like compelling them to do or to give something regardless of their will. It's like leaving them without a choice but to give you what you want. So how can we refrain from demanding and start requesting? This one is not that hard to do. It has been just about change on the pitch and change on lyrics.

Instead of saying "give me that" you can say "please", or "may you give me that?" It's just simple right? If you think yes, it isn't just about that. The way of asking or requesting something is to be considered also. You have to do that in the most romantic tone that you can. You don't have to sound like begging but just enough to show that you are not demanding but requesting.

Start by providing reasons why we want or need that something should follow. Your partner should understand why you are requesting for it. If you will be able to explain the reason, then your partner might probably grant your request. I believe our partners would always love to provide us everything we want or need provided that it will not be harmful or inimical to us or our relationship with them. If you request for something that your partner may not be able to give you like a permission to attend a casino with friends for some bonding moment, make your partner understand your point. Never shout or carry any angry tone, (this is how we, guys, often react when our desire is not permitted) remember you are requesting.

What if your partner can't really be able to give what you ask? If for some valid reason this happens, do not frown in front of your partner. Tell yourself this one, "Everything happens for a reason." Yes everything occurs for a certain purpose. Who might know, your partner doesn't permit to go with your friends to bound in a casino but she contacted your friends for you to have party at home or elsewhere. If your reason is the bonding time with your friends then that will be solved. If otherwise, then you should've told your partner your real motive.

Communication is definitely one of the keys to add or re-ignite sparks in a relationship. A good communication means sound relationship. Everything in the context of relationship needs to be communicated. It is not bad to request for something we want or need. You must remember that in a relationship you are two. You both have to complete each other by understanding and giving way to one another.

REMIND YOUR PARTNER HOW GREAT SHE IS

Have you ever been asked the question, “Why do you love me?” How did you respond? Sometimes our loved ones get curious as to why we chose them over others. The question can seem easy to answer by plainly describing the good things about our partners. We may say “because you are awesome, beautiful, and loyal,” “because your sense of humor is terrific,” or “because you cook the best.” In reality, those are the things we see in them but aren’t the real reason why we love them, right? I believe that love travels on invisible waves that no one can see or touch; therefore, no one can explain it, and so no reason can be given why we’re feeling it. If you are able to give your partner a reason, then it is the reason for your attraction but never for your love.

Though we don’t need any particular reason to love someone, aside from truly feeling it in our heart, we still feel flattered and happy when our partners provide us with reasons why they love us. This shows us that our partner appreciates those things in us. It also indicates that his or her feelings are true, for they have a basis, and as long as we possess the characteristics that they love about us, they will never leave us.

More than providing these feelings, this also signifies contentment and appreciation. Who wouldn't feel on cloud 9 if he, or his work, was appreciated? I would say no one. Reminding your partner about how great he or she is is probably one of the best things any person should practice. When should you do it? You don't have to wait for something as a signal to remind you of your partner's great qualities.

Start by complimenting her every morning with your greetings. Tell her how beautiful she is with her uncombed hair and nightgown. Though it might sound like a jest, believe me, there will be some tickling power that will trigger her lips to smile. Tell her how good her cooking is, or her voice when she's singing while cooking, and that that is just one reason why you love her. Again, the intention is not to make her believe it, because she may not. It is to put a smile on her face, and more smiles day by day. Tell her how gorgeous she looks in whatever clothes she wears; remember, girls always want to be beautiful in their partner's eyes. Whenever you can think of something to say to please her, grab the opportunity. Don't be bothered by her reaction; as long as you are able to make her smile, you are on the right track.

This act of reminding your partner about how great she is may open a wider avenue for good things to happen. It could be the start of many light and healthy conversations. This will allow you to make her feel special in a simple way. It will also allow you to smile together, and that is one of the sweetest kind of moments partners can share.

PLAY A STRIP GAME

Couples' relationships can be amazingly improved if the two partners add a little variety to their intimacy. This can be achieved in a very simple way - by playing strip games. People who choose to have fun in this way can gain many advantages in their relationship. Getting naked playing such games can be very entertaining as well. The two of you will be enticed into bed together easily. Do you think that you are not very creative when it comes to strip games? Here are some examples of games that you can turn into strip games.

For instance, you and your partner can play strip Twister. Whoever loses a round has to take off a piece of clothing. At some point, you will forget the game and will fall into each other's arms – maybe literally. Another game you can try together is strip chess, especially because it is a game played by two people. Every time a partner loses a chess piece, he/she must take off one piece of clothing. You may not finish the actual game, because it will make you eager to “finish” in a different way!

Monopoly also can be turned into a strip game full of fun. All you need to do is to change some of the rules. When a player must pay the bank, rather than using their fake money, they can give up a piece of clothing. Whenever someone wins money, he or she has the right to recover a clothing item instead. Trying to recover clothes can be very entertaining. Another game that you can use as a pretext to get naked is this simple one: First, you must think of a number. Then ask your partner to guess that number. If he or she doesn’t guess correctly, or maybe even if he/she does, you can say: "That’s not the number I was thinking of!" The rule of the game is that whoever doesn’t guess the number has to take off a piece of clothing. And again, the fun is guaranteed!

For better success with these games, you can create a special atmosphere with candles and appropriate music. This will help make things more romantic and appealing. You could also follow the game with a slow dance while listening to your favorite music. The rest, of course, is predictable!

Everyone loves to play. Why don't you use a strip game as a way to get closer to your partner’s heart? It will be fun and exciting at the same time. It is a very pleasant way to spend time with your loved one. And the biggest advantage of a strip game is that it improves a couple's sexual relationship. In this way you will banish the monotony, you will make your partner eager for a night of love, and it will help you to show more interest than before as well. All you need to do is to be inventive and brave!

HOLDING HANDS IN PUBLIC

While there are many techniques to keep the fire burning in a relationship, one that won't fail is to step out of the box and do things that neither one of you would normally do. Another effective move is to go back to doing the things you did when the relationship was fresh - like holding hands while in public.

Wherever you are when you do it, the sure thing is that holding hands is an activity that strengthens a relationship, if not also serving as a declaration of ownership. It is a natural phenomenon for those in love.

Remember walking around with your partner when you were dating and just enjoying the fact that you were with that someone special? Back then, that person was new, and you still had a lot to learn about him. He was to be conquered, and every gesture of affection counted: tender kisses, lovely looks, cute whispers… It was all about being romantic and winning that someone new. But then as time went by, it's possible that you may have gotten used to having that someone by your side, and you forgot how amazing that person is, or maybe you just forget to show it now. So try doing all that stuff you used to do:

First, go to a simple place such as a park, walk around, and remember – it's not about the place you're at; it's about the person you're with and the relationship. So hold hands and just walk around. Never mind if it seems awkward to both of you. Walking around may get the two of you to talk. A simple chat may work wonders; try not to talk about work or the subjects you normally discuss. If talking doesn't come naturally or easily to you, then give the following option a try.

Don't look around, but focus on the feeling of the hand you're holding; focus on the person who's holding your hand. Just hold and focus till the awkwardness disappears. Holding hands is a tender gesture; it reminds you of the link you have with that someone, and it shows the rest of the world there is a bond between the two of you.

Holding hands while you're going shopping may be tricky, but it will also help you to bond. Being in a relationship is about finding happiness together, so if you have to go to different stores, go together and be there with each other. If you're out to dinner, let go of your cell phone and instead hold each other's hand, which will help you focus on the person and the moment you're sharing.

A lot of the trouble in relationships starts when couples begin to drift apart, whether it's due to work or friends or other activities. Take some time for each other and just focus on your relationship; as the two of you reconnect, the intimacy will start flowing, and before you know it you'll be back on the road of passion.

TREAT YOUR PARTNER AS IF YOU MET HIM OR HER YESTERDAY

The most typical mistake is to assume that we know everything there is to know. The first rule about learning is to understand that there's always something more you can learn. This rule applies to romance as well: after you've been dating someone for a while, or living with that someone, certain habits and patterns start to emerge. It's then when you might get the idea that you already know everything there is to know about that someone. When this happens you might start to get bored, but in case you didn't know, "Boredom is just a waste of your creativity."

The people around you are full of surprises; as humans, we change daily. It's the basic rule of life: in order to survive we must adapt, and adaptation implies change. We learn daily from what happens around us, and even the lessons we have already learned sometimes reappear in our lives.

So, if you've been with someone for a while, my recommendation for you is to try looking at that person as if you had only just met him or her. It's not about pretending to forget everything you know, although that could be a great step for reviving the passion. But if amnesia is not on the map, and I hope it's not, you can simply try to look at your partner from a new perspective, giving yourself the opportunity to learn things you didn't know about him/her.

Most often the basic questions, such as what is his favorite color or what would he do if he faced a certain ethical dilemma, might lead you to learn something new about him and refresh your whole relationship. Sometimes as we get to know other people we create prejudices about them, and we assume things, about which we might be wrong. So getting to know your partner again is a great opportunity for you to revive the flames and to lay a new and stronger foundation in the relationship.

Start by developing the attitude that, no matter how many years you have spent together, you are still a stranger to your partner.

New beginnings will in fact help you fix some of the troubles you may be having, they will help you and your partner get to know each other again, and they will bring you closer so you can reawaken the fire. Since we are all changing all the time, treating each other as if you had just met is not so crazy after all.

DON'T GO TO BED ANGRY WITH EACH OTHER

Conflicts arise in a relationship; they're normal for normal partners. There are several levels of severity in conflicts. The more severe they are, the longer it takes to resolve them, but do you believe that the most severe conflict that should be permitted in a relationship is the one that will last for a day only? Have you experienced a disagreement with your partner? How did you settle it?

We humans end each day in bed. If we want to keep the spark in our relationship, then we shouldn't close our days angry with each other. When you go to bed and let the night pass still angry with each other, nothing will change the next day, which will mean that much time was wasted on your anger. Would you want that to happen?

So how do we end conflicts before the day closes? If a problem arises early in the day, you have plenty of time to resolve it; but if it rises in the middle of the day or later, how will you reconcile before bedtime?

Actually, the time of day the conflict arises is not important when the focus is on settling it. What matters most is your drive to end the dispute between you and your partner. The first thing that always pops into our mind when we quarrel with our partner is probably the question of who is in the wrong or who caused the problem. Most of the time you are not ready to admit that you were wrong; that's natural. So who's flawed now? Finding faults in your partner won't fix the problem. You are just trying to lift the guilt from you. Instead of asking who is at fault, you have to ask yourself what you can do to help yourself and your partner forget whatever went wrong and reconcile. The next thing you have to do is to make the first move. Keep in mind that in a relationship, the one who first approaches the other and first says sorry is not always the one who is to blame but rather the one who loves more.

Gain the will to make the first move by considering the following things. Which is more important, your ego or your partner? Which do you prefer, anger or love? Which of these would you rather have: sweet dreams with your loved one or lonely, sleepless nights without your partner by your side? These few simple questions can drive you to make the first move. Guys are forever and always suitors. We are tasked to court our partners from the very first moment we are attracted to them until our dying day, and for suitors, ending a misunderstanding can be done in the most simple but romantic way. We are blessed with a brain full of silly ideas that are always capable of capturing our queen's heart, so use that brain. The last thing you have to do after settling a matter is to talk about it. Your partner might say "Let's just not talk about it," but you must insist.

Talking about how and why it started, stating your side, listening to your partner and meeting halfway are the methods that help keep conflicts from happening again. The purpose of this article is not to set up a barrier to keep out any future conflicts that may arise. No words can have control over that. The real purpose is to make you see problems in a relationship as problems that are meant to be solved to keep the relationship going and sparkling.

ACCEPT THE THINGS THAT YOU CANNOT CHANGE

It can be difficult to accept things you don't want. It's even harder if those things are involved in your relationship. The reality is that there will always be things that you don't want in almost every part of your surroundings. Oftentimes, these things can become a threat to your relationship.

When things go wrong or start to get out of control and you're badly aware of this and dislike them, acceptance is the key you need to deal with your circumstances. You may be faced with several situations over which you have no control, and so you just have to accept them. In dealing with our partners, we must tolerate certain things that we cannot change about them. It isn't easy to just swallow everything being fed to you, but there are a few things that you can do to learn to accept unpleasant circumstances.

First, use your partner as inspiration to accept undesirable things. Remember the adage: where there is a will, there is a way. Suppose you once told your partner that with him/her you can do anything; or if you have never said that to him/her, then say it now and start proving it. In order to have the will to accept things, you have to be open-minded. Before accepting anything, though, first accept the fact that the world is not perfect. Imperfections are not only present in the things you don't like, but also in you. If you want to be accepted even though you are not perfect, then you must learn to accept others' imperfections too.

The next step is to talk about the things you dislike. You and your partner must sit down and discuss them openly. This will allow you to see things from a different perspective, and hopefully you can learn to appreciate them, or at least to accept and live with them. You may not see something with as much clarity as your partner does, so if you talk about it, you might come to realize the essence of that something as perceived by another. Once you and your partner have discussed a matter, you have to start learning to get used to it. You might have been ignoring that something or were in denial about it right from the start. Now start to live with it. This is the gateway of acceptance. Don't close off your senses when you encounter that something. Get used to it. If you are starting with it, it's time for the final touch.

Accepting things we don't want but can't change can be really onerous, but it is not impossible. It is like running toward something in the far distance that we eventually will reach. This requires effort from both parties in the relationship: from the one who's making the effort to accept something, and from the one who'll inspire him or her in this endeavor. Almost every person has to play one or both of these roles; it is just the nature of our imperfect world.

The sure thing is that, in order to have a happy and productive life, we all need to embrace each other's imperfection.

NEVER GIVE UP ON SHOWING THAT YOU CARE

A beautiful relationship does not depend on how good of an understanding we have with someone. It depends on how well we avoid misunderstandings, since we all have an unlimited capacity to love. To love is our true nature. Yet love can be the thing that is missed in our lives. We have become the victims of circumstances. The stress of modern living is slowly and silently depriving us of our natural attributes. Love begets love. The more you shower love on others, the more receptive you become to others' love. However, nature teaches us to give love unconditionally. Expressing and demonstrating our love is as important as feeling love.

Man is a psychological being, not just a physical one. He loves to be loved. A relationship needs to be nurtured in order to blossom and to last long. When you care for your loved ones, you need to make them "see" and "feel" your love.

Caring for someone is an ongoing process. Time is a crucial factor in the process of caring and loving. **T.I.M.E.** is an acronym for: **Think** over the importance of caring and being aware of a need, **Identify** the things that waste time and keep you away from your near-and-dear ones, **Make** a list of things you can do to effectively exhibit your love and care, and **Establish** priorities in your life. It is here that your conviction and commitment will come to play a pivotal role. Chalk out a program. Decide how much more time you can squeeze into your busy schedule to spend with your family. Rest assured that you are spending enough time as long as you are spending quality time.

You should make it a habit to engage all members of the family in conversation, and make sure that there is a mutual exchange of how you feel towards each other. Show that you care, not just by spending time talking with them, but by listening to all their problems. Never giving up means insisting on demonstrating your feelings of love even if you are condemned, judged or un-appreciated. Continue to nurture what you believe is good for the relationship and what you think will show your care.

Every relationship is like a glass. A scratch on one side will reflect on the other side. So always handle everyone with care. Let love flow from you in abundance. When there is a caring person around, others will turn more and more towards him or her to ease their physical, mental and emotional stress. Be that person who can be their emotional anchor for life. Ensure a high degree of consistency in your behavior and attitude. Thus, how much of your love and concern you express is what will make it worthwhile. Only expressed love is acknowledged and reciprocated.

GIVE EACH OTHER SOME SPACE

Sometimes in a committed relationship, it is difficult to remember your individuality. People who have been together for a while tend to rely on their partners heavily, but this sort of reliance can be too much weight for some to carry. If you have access to cable TV or have seen a romantic comedy recently, you must have heard this cliché: *If you love someone, let them go. It's true that a butterfly will only land in an open hand; however, a grip is easier to tighten than to loosen.*

Allowing your partner some space helps reestablish his or her sense of self. Knowing how to do it in the right way is the key to this tip, though. A sense of self is important to establish, though it is not suggested that you take a break or begin any sort of open relationship. Just try to create a little distance, while continuing to be committed to each other. Following is a three-step process based on confrontation, separation, and reevaluation. All these will help you rediscover the early days of your relationship.

The first step is all about telling your partner how you feel. To say the least, this is a very delicate conversation to have. The trick here is to be honest and tactful. Honesty isn't too difficult, but being tactful has always been a challenge. How do you tell someone you love that it's time for some space? It is important to review all that has been happening and explain why a little breathing room could help end this rough patch. Don't drop the classic breakup line, "It's not you, it's me." You are just going to take a vacation for a while to get a fresh view on the world; don't be so dramatic over everything. This could help you rediscover who you are as an individual.

If this is something your partner agrees to, you'll need to know how to discover your individuality again. Watch what you want to watch on TV, get involved again in the activities you've had to sacrifice because of your partner, and spend time just reflecting on who you'd like to be. Really, this step is all about you. Don't stray from your relationship during this time of separation; instead, consider what you appreciate about your relationship.

Re-evaluation is the last step. As you've been considering who you are alone, now consider what you both bring to your relationship. Think about how to make your relationship better for both of your personalities, and make it happen.

Separation is always scary, and the longer you have been together, the harder it will be. However, it can be one of the healthiest steps you take to build a better relationship. As long as you treat the situation as delicately as possible, you can't go wrong. Remember, the steps are designed to help you do this, so don't skimp on any of them. Some of the best decisions you make together are based on what you have learned apart.

HAVE A POSITIVE ATTITUDE!

Be the captain of your life. Here is one open secret that will help you reach heights. Yes, you are right; it is to maintain a positive attitude. This will enable you to have a balanced perspective as to your goals in life. It will keep your life going smoothly with minimal hardships. In fact, someone who keeps up a positive attitude is never hit by the so-called *hard things* in life. To him, they are just another experience in life.

Our altitude is the result of our attitude and not our aptitude. You may have a good job, a high salary, the best circle of friends and a loving family. But if you lack a positive attitude, you cannot reap benefits from them; love will present a gloomy picture devoid of fun and charm, and peace and happiness will elude you. If you already possess a positive attitude, make efforts to maintain it and polish it. Never become complacent. If you are plagued by a negative attitude, then it is time you make every effort to come out of it. Streamline your thoughts. Time and tide wait for no one.

First and foremost, love your own self. Develop a positive self-image. No one can make you feel inferior without your consent. Take an objective view on life. Start focusing on the important matters, and leave trivial issues behind. Do not expect things to change for you. When you change, then things change in your favor. Remember that people will think of you in the manner you want them to. Concentrate on your skills and winning qualities. Each one of us has them. All we need to do is to identify them and stimulate them. Stay cool. Do not allow stress to damage your physical and mental health.

Once you have perfected such an attitude, you can start influencing your partner with your positivity. Influencing doesn't mean forcing your partner to have that attitude. It's all about showing him/her the benefits of having such a positive attitude and keeping it that way. You may struggle with this process. However, you should note that the fruits of your labor will be sweet. Learn from others who energize you with their positivity.

Both positivity and negativity are contagious. Keep the right company to develop the right traits. What we believe determines how we feel. The way we feel influences our actions. Negative thoughts are like parasites that drain our energy. So you must purposefully drive out negative thoughts and adorn your mind with optimism.

All people are the same, except for one little difference that makes all the difference. The little difference is attitude, and the big difference is whether it is positive or not. Our negative thoughts fuel a negative mindset, which takes control of our life, making it miserable. Thinking positive thoughts will remove all negative traces from your mind, as where there is light there is no room for darkness. We have a choice: to live like a slave or a master. Let positivity flow from every pore of your existence. Positive thoughts give rise to positive words and deeds. Our positivity must inspire our family members. You will be a desirable influence on everyone, including your partner.

HAVING A DRINK TOGETHER IN THE BACKYARD

One great secret to a happy relationship is to enjoy a drink or two together. Whether you drink frequently or not, this activity works best at night. Studies have shown that couples who enjoy a cocktail or two together from time to time have better intimacy and handle their problems more easily than those who consume drinks apart or those who don't drink at all. An essential condition for this process to be successful is that you and your partner stay sober because a higher consumption of alcoholic beverages can lead to more problems in your relationship.

You've never had a drink with your loved one before? It's time to try this recipe, and you might reap more benefits than you expect. So, after dinner, invite your life partner out to the backyard to have a drink together. It's not necessary that a candlelit scene be served up; the farther away you are from romanticism, the more natural things become to both of you.

The first advantage that you will get from this experience is that you will both have the opportunity to communicate more with each other. Moderate drinking is known to make all your inhibitions disappear and give you the necessary courage to express your true thoughts and feelings. Thus, after having a cocktail together in the silence of your backyard, you and your partner will be able to tell each other things that you could not say otherwise. You will be able to say to your lover, "You have gorgeous eyes!" or maybe you will hear from him or her, "I love you so much!" It could be something that your partner has been longing to tell you but has avoided saying because you might get hurt, like a review of your attitude as a partner. Good thing you're a little drunk to absorb that; look on the bright side of those words that have been hidden for years.

Another benefit of moderate alcohol consumption together with your life partner is the improvement of your intimacy. Drinking small quantities of alcoholic beverages makes partners become closer to one another physically and pushes them into bed together more quickly. After you enjoy a mild drink together in the backyard, it will be no surprise for you to wind up in one another's arms, whispering words of love to each other and heading for your spousal bedroom hand in hand. Not to mention the courage that both of you will gain in bed! The drink will help you to be more willing to accept each other's fantasies and to offer more pleasure to each other.

No matter how good it may seem to you to have a drink together with your partner, you should not forget one thing: you must not exceed your limits. What is encouraged here is just to have a small drink to get fired up, not only in bed but for expressing your ideas and - more importantly - your feelings to your partner. Drinking together is a sign of sharing one another's pain and happiness in a glass. You should try it sometime.

GIVE EACH OTHER SOME BREATHING ROOM

Marriages are made in heaven and managed at home. Fights or boredom are a revelation that something in your relationship needs to be strengthened. There are times in all relationships when things do not work out as planned or expected. Well, every relationship has its share of ups and downs. The reasons can range from having conflicting expectations to being distracted by other issues to having difficulty expressing your feelings in a way that others understand. Giving each other some breathing space is the key to renewed love and affection, as distance makes one grow fonder.

Everyone craves personal space. We want to pamper ourselves. Why not give that privilege to our partner? Why not give him or her some adequate personal space?

Doing so will breathe fresh life into your relationship. It will relieve you from the boredom and monotony of an uneventful, unfulfilling, and unmotivated lifestyle. It is essential for every normal, healthy person and relationship. You can start giving your partner some space by being less possessive of him/her. Possessiveness shuts off one's creativity. Do not try to control his time and activities or monitor his every move. It could make him uneasy and uncomfortable.

Secondly, never engage in emotional blackmailing like insisting that your partner spend all his time with you, give up past friends, or wear clothes of your choice. Don't force him to relate to your kith and kin or insist that he join and develop rapport with your circle of friends. All this creates pressure and can make your partner feel choked. He will be physically present but mentally absent, giving plastic smiles and nods. It will make his life miserable. Every time you do things like this, it will rupture your ties a little more.

To give some positive advice, try putting yourself in your partner's shoes. Think with fairness and justice. Behave like mature adults. Some personal breathing space offers respite from your stress-filled workload and helps you to recharge your batteries. Take time to ponder, contemplate, and analyze. It will have a soothing effect. It clears your mind, releases all pent up emotions, and enables you to think more logically. Take a break from mundane chores.

You need it, and so does your partner. Give him a break while you take a break too. This tender and considerate gesture will be reciprocated. Time spent apart will make time spent together more enjoyable. It improves your attitude and mood. You will be raring to go.

Variety is the spice of life. Savor every moment together and apart. Take time to rediscover yourself. This will motivate and refresh you. Harmonious and balanced partners make for a strong relationship. Give him the space he craves, and then together you can reap its benefits.

BE A TALKER

In any couple's relationship, communication is one of the most important issues, perhaps the most important of all. When the two people talk more with each other, they clarify different situations that may occur, find the best solutions for their problems and get to understand one another better. If one partner chooses to hide his/her thoughts and feelings from the other, this will make that person accumulate a lot of tension and frustration, which will be expressed most often when fighting.

Why wait until we get to that point? Just because we don't know how to communicate our feelings and assume the other can guess our thoughts? It's not justifiable, so talk now.

When it comes to talking, those who tend to talk more are women. They think they are good at communicating and, if something goes wrong in their relationship, they often blame their partner because he does not talk as much. Men, on the other hand, think of themselves as good speakers, only they communicate just what is important. Most of the time, it is sad to say, men get annoyed listening to their girlfriends'/wives' woes and, sometimes, pointless ideas. This affects many relationships. What is required, in this case, for both partners is to find suitable solutions in order to have better communication. This is not what we want, so you must be able to distinguish what is too much from what we need from you.

First, women need to be aware of and accept the fact that men are less communicative than they are. It is true that there are men who talk more, but these are rare cases. What a woman can do in order to have better communication with her partner is to talk whenever two things happen. The first thing is when conditions are a little heated and gloomy. Say what you think immediately. Unaddressed feelings will grow silently in the dark and will be nourished by a broken heart. The second thing is to talk when everything is okay. Here you can choose a topic that captures your partner's attention. Think of something interesting. Always paint a happy picture for both of you and never stop trying even if troubles come your way.

Try to reach out to your partner. If he begins to talk, then things will go smoothly and you'll get closer to each other.

Whether you are male or female, you have to know that talking brings many benefits to your relationship. When partners speak to each other, they may say important things and, at the same time, communicate a persona. It is good to let your life partner know what you are thinking, how you feel, and what you want, so that he/she will know how to act in order to make you happy. Do not choose to put up a wall between you.

NO FAMILY INTERFERENCE

The extended family can sometimes become a real nightmare for a couple, but there are methods you can use to prevent an overload of familial interference. The ultimate secret is that, whenever necessary, you must protect your relationship at all costs from your family's intrusion.

All couples need to have their own rules for their relationship to work. Any intrusion coming from other people, even those who are close to you, such as parents, sisters or brothers, can affect your balance at certain times. The discomfort you feel then is normal because, although in most cases relatives have good intentions, only you know what the best solution for your relationship is. Moreover, independence from the rest of the family is an important condition for the survival of any relationship.

Parents and parents-in-law may be under the impression that it is their duty to take care of you even though you're fully-grown adults and can solve problems on your own.

They probably don't even realize that, by giving you too many tips and interfering too much, they are just putting extra pressure on your relationship. The only ones who can correct this attitude are you two, and things will work out if you follow some rules. So start by creating a list of do's and don'ts.

Yes, set some rules and respect them. Explain to your partner the benefits of setting rules and respecting individuality. This may not sound so appealing to him or her, but history will repeat itself and patterns will continue into the future unless you change them. More and more couples are having problems because of family intervention and comments on what you should do and how you should act. Tell your partner that you still appreciate his/her family's dedication and you're aware that that "careful" attitude comes from their affection. Make sure you send this message clearly. Do not make it sound like those relatives are bad people. Help your partner to be rational about things that come up, and emphasize that your priority is saving this relationship from anyone's aggressive or inappropriate involvement.

Why there is a need to do this? For one example, as a basic illustration, it is because mothers-in-law tend to find different causes, real or imagined, as excuses for their aversion towards their daughters-in-law. The true reason for the tensions that arise is that, in general, mothers-in-law do not easily accept their new status, and they can perceive their daughter-in-law as a rival competing for their son's affection. In this way, they can create countless tensions and say harsh words not only to their son's wife, but also even to their own son. In such situations, it is necessary that the daughter-in-law and her husband form a common front. The man will have to explain to his mother that her attitude towards his wife affects him and that he loves them both, but in different ways. At the same time, the daughter-in-law will have to prove she has the wisdom not to respond aggressively to the inequities of the mother-in-law. This is also true with the woman's family. This is the kind of scenario that you have to plan for with your partner.

The more you have the chance to create your own space for your relationship, the easier it is to avoid the possible interference of family in your life and possible fights in the future. You must set clear rules together and follow them together as well.

If you and your partner take separate viewpoints and actions in this area, parents and in-laws may interpret that as a sign of weakness in the relationship and may try to intervene, and this could confuse the relationship even more. You should treat your parents-in-law with all the respect that you are able to give and should let them know with certainty that your purpose is not to separate them from their son/daughter.

SAY NO TO SECRETS

Do you have a hidden agenda in your marriage? It is only a matter of time before the secret is out. We enter into a marriage alliance to seek fulfillment. Your relationship should go beyond just romance and sex and should be built on a foundation of intimacy and contentment. You should work together towards a deeper, sharing, open and honest relationship.

Many couples lead a life devoid of deep and intimate conversation. Their relationship is one of silence and emotional estrangement where intimate feelings are kept inside, unshared with their partner. You should open up about your flaws; that is the way to a healthier you and a healthier relationship. Hiding a part of you is deceiving your partner, which impedes intimacy between and your partner. It will only cause harm for both of you. Remember that the heart that loves dearly is hurt deeply when flooded with secrets.

It is impossible to sustain a marriage without complete transparency on the part of both spouses. Secrets are the royal road to misunderstanding, suspicion and distrust. Secrets are heavy and wear us down. Men can hide loans, while women may also hide incurred losses. Keeping such secrets has unpleasant and dangerous consequences. It erodes the foundations of the institution of marriage and its values.

Couples should be able to talk and plan together. An ideal relationship is one based on mutual love, trust and respect. The formula, actually, is simple; you just have to be loyal to your partner, and the secret to that is that genuine communication should be placed at the center of good relationships. A secret, moreover, does not necessarily mean that you are hiding something bad. It could just be a failure of yours or something else you refuse to talk about. Reveal the truth, because a heart that loves you will accept you and everything about you.

Revealing a secret means trusting, and it requires good timing on your part. Don't just blurt out everything rashly because you have found the courage to say it. Before you divulge it, you have to make sure that your partner is in the mood to absorb and deal with that secret you've been keeping for the last three months. Your partner may become wary and wonder why you have just now told him this. Well, that is not an unexpected reaction. You just have to bear with the consequences. After all, you have had little lapses. You should also refrain from overreacting to your partner's response. Your reaction might throw more fuel on the fire if he or she is angry, which is something we warn you not to do.

Having clarity about what to share and what not to share is a basic communication skill that all couples should learn and use for a successful married life. Share a secret at the appropriate time. Maintain a transparent, happy, and healthy marriage. Sharing secrets actually heals and strengthens the bonds in relationships.

Have you seen a barrier come down between two people after one of them has revealed a secret? It is the same way in a marriage relationship. Yes, telling the truth breaks down barriers and leads you to a new level of acceptance, and it adds authenticity to the relationship.

MAKE UP AFTER A FIGHT

Differences of opinion need not destroy a marriage. The best attitude to resolve a fight is to think in terms of "we" and "us" instead of "I" and "you." Convert an obstacle into an opportunity. Even the most ideal marriages have their share of tiffs and showdowns. The secret of successful couples is not having the right "chemistry" between the two partners. It is how they handle conflict that makes all the difference. Good communication between partners is the key to a happy, lasting marriage.

Let us start by reconnecting. This process will help you to grasp where you stand on something. Ask yourself after a fight, "Is this argument worth holding onto and not resolving now?"

If your answer is yes, then go with it and suffer the consequences later in the life of your relationship. If it's no, then start with these pieces of advice. Give up on crabbing about the past. Live, fight, forgive, forget and live again. That is the formula for a happy and lasting marriage. Fights are inevitable, but what we can control is that we should learn from an argument. Start the mending process now and every time after you fight. I know it is hard since you will not be in the mood to do it at those times, but give it a try when the hurt from that fight has lessened a little. Make it your primary motive to patch up and replenish your togetherness. Reconnect yourself to rationality.

The second step is to channel your thoughts into your words and deeds on the road to a perfect marriage. Start focusing on what is important to you. Look beneath an argument. The root cause of a difference in opinion should be identified and addressed. Life is definitely not a practice run, and you should be well aware that time and tide wait for no one. So take the first step before stagnation sets in. Take responsibility to keep the marriage ticking by making the first move back toward your partner.

Stay cool. Never fall prey to negative feelings. A negative attitude brings along ugliness and bitterness in its wake. Let your attitude be a positive one that promotes new life and growth and other positive outcomes. Like you, no one likes to be taken for granted. Everyone seeks recognition and appreciation.

Love can conquer all. Time is the greatest healer of all pains and conflicts. Shove issues "under the rug" that are not addressable. Make repairing attempts. Prevent conflicts from escalating. Mending things between you is the best thing to do after intense arguments. It serves as water to douse the fire that could destroy both of you. Act now, for you might regret it later if you don't. Making up after a fight is a vital skill to revive your lost connection. Your willingness and effort will make things better and ensure lasting happiness and togetherness.

VOLUNTEER TOGETHER!

Becoming a volunteer for a particular organization is, usually, a wonderful thing for a person to do. Offering your time is a fantastic pastime. It is truly awesome to offer your help to other people without expecting anything in return. But there are also many benefits that volunteering can give a person who practices it. Some of them are: increasing self-esteem, acquiring experience, getting to know new people and new things, and more. If you like the idea of volunteering, what if, instead of becoming a volunteer by yourself, you also brought your partner into the activity? Wouldn't it be a great thing for both of you?

Are you wondering how you could do this? There are a few steps you need to follow for success in this approach. First of all, you have to establish what kind of activity you wish to be involved in. There are many ways to volunteer: You can choose to participate in charitable activities for poor people, or you can get involved in charitable actions for the environment. Alternatively, you could opt to do mentoring activities, such as helping children to read better. It is important to choose a kind of activity that you both can do with pleasure.

Then, you need to find an organization that will provide you all the information you need. The next step is to get to work: all you have to do is to offer some of your free time in order to help those in need. You will enjoy two great advantages: first – you will get to try something new that you haven't done before, and second – you will get to spend quality time together with your partner. In this way you will have the opportunity to get to know one another in a different situation, to see how your life partner reacts when he or she is providing support for a worthy cause. It is possible to discover new and different things about the person you love. And this, in turn, gives your partner the opportunity to get to know you better. Surely both of you will learn a lot from such an experience!

Everyone should get involved in volunteer action. Doing good things for other people makes you feel better. And if you choose to volunteer with your life partner, this is a double win. Volunteering reveals positive aspects of a person, making him/her more generous and more careful with his/her fellows. When a couple gets involved in a charitable activity together, both partners will grow lovelier in one another's eyes. Each of them will see qualities in the other person that they hadn't discovered before, and this will bring the two partners closer. Isn't it great that you can do useful things together with the one you love? You can start this as soon as possible, and you will soon see that this experience will bring wonderful benefits to your relationship!

HAVE DINNER IN THE COMPANY OF A HAPPY COUPLE!

It is known that emotions are easily transmitted from one person to another, so they can be contagious. It is much harder to be happy in an environment where people are negatively influencing each other. Unhappiness can spread to everyone. It is therefore very important that the two of you spend your time around some people who try to provide wonderful feelings to others, because it is very possible for you to become like them. You can discover several occasions to meet couples who are friends of yours and have a successful relationship. In this way, you have the chance to learn a lot of things from them.

One opportunity is to invite a happy couple to dine with you. Having dinner with your life partner can often be a romantic time when you can share your feelings. But after a while this can become boring. Why don't you try another experience: having dinner with a couple like you? You will have more joy and fun. If you don't really know how to do it, here are some steps that might help you.

First, you need to agree on the date when you wish to have this get-together. It is necessary for each one of you to make time in your schedule for such an experience. Weekends are the best! Then you must decide where you'll have the meal - you can suggest someplace or you may ask the other couple which place works best for them. What is important is that you pick a location that all of you will enjoy. Once these details have been established, all that's left is to get ready for the dinner.

Having dinner with another couple can be a really good way to perk up your relationship. You have the opportunity to get to know other people's ways of thinking and reacting; you can borrow healthy habits from those people. Also, the happiness of the couple can become transmitted to you. It is possible to have some things that are not very good in your relationship; however, you can learn from another couple. Maybe it's the way they talk with each other, or maybe it's the way they smile, or maybe their jokes make the relationship more interesting. There are many positive things that you can learn from a happy couple and apply in your own relationship.

It is enough to enjoy the company of two people who love each other, even just for one get-together. But you will probably want to repeat this experience again and again. All you need to do is to have the necessary disposition to meet such people and to learn new things that will strengthen your relationship. You will feel much better after you witness a relationship other than your own. Then you will be able to evaluate things, to analyze how your relationship is compared to others'. You will only learn and grow from this experience!

INVITE YOUR PARENTS TO DINNER AND COOK FOR THEM TOGETHER!

Life partners can perform many activities together. Some of them are in the category of necessary things, and others are the fun ones. But one activity that can be both useful and enjoyable is to cook together. Often cooking alone can be boring. That's why it would be great for the two of you to spend quality time together preparing a nice dinner. But this dinner doesn't have to be an ordinary one; you can invite your parents, for example, to make it a little more special. This will motivate both of you to do the best cooking job you can.

But how can you prepare this event? First, you have to invite your parents over for dinner. It would be great for both your parents and your partner's parents to be present. After you get confirmation that they will come, you two can get to work. It is very important to prepare this dinner together and not just have one of you do it. The purpose of the activity is to bring you closer, so make it happen. You will see that preparing such an event will draw you closer to each other. You will have the opportunity to help one another, to form a team. Second, it will be necessary to set the menu. You will have to make sure you cook something that everyone will love. Third, once you have established what you will cook, you need to divide up the responsibilities: who will prepare the steak, or who will make the stuffing, etc. That way you will be more organized and will finish everything much faster.

If you are not used to cooking together, you will see how enjoyable this activity can be! Each of you will have a chance to ask the other for suggestions, like: "How much pepper should I put in this?" or "What flavor should the cake be?”

When everything is ready and your guests arrive, tell them how you have prepared the meal. This will be an opportunity for fun conversation for all of you. Especially for people who don't know how to cook very well. This can be a real challenge. While eating dinner, you can tell your parents the funny moments you had while preparing it. Such an event will bring you closer to one another, but it will also bring you closer to your family. Surely it will be a dinner that you won't forget!

It is very nice to participate in many different activities as a couple. Food brings people together. Why not bring the two of you together preparing it? Cooking together with your partner will help you do things better and faster, as everybody could use a helping hand. At the same time, it will transform the two of you into a wonderful team – you will see how nice it is to make something important together!

SEPARATE TOILETRIES

We hear lovers making tall statements that they love each other so much that they even share the same toothbrush. Hopefully their love remains even after the brush wears out. Sharing toiletries should not be considered a sign of demonstrating love. Mature couples arrive at the right balance between sharing and separating. It is ideal and wise to have separate and personal sets of toiletries, as each person is unique in his or her needs and prefers products that cater to his/her individual taste and needs.

We all dream of having a flourishing relationship. But sharing toiletries is a sure cause of friction.

Why?

Many women are toiletry hoarders. Their stash can include big bottled hygiene products like body soap, toothpaste and a toothbrush, shampoo and conditioner, sunscreen for summer and moisturizer for winter, small things like nail clippers, tweezers, files and dental floss, all different kinds of makeup, and the list goes on. Aside from that, most women love to spend more time freshening up than men do. On the opposite end of the spectrum, some men hold the opinion that spending time on hygiene and appearance is something for only the opposite sex to be concerned with. This attitude to such an essential aspect of living is both unhealthy and immature. There is a thin line separating neglect and obsession.

Another strong reason for couples not to share toiletries is to avoid smelling alike. This will make the relationship uninteresting. Over time, when couples use the same soap and shampoo, which is seemingly a very small and unimportant detail in your shower, it can have a big impact on your relationship. Think about it. Doesn't it sound logical? To some people it may not, but would you still want to lie down next to your partner who smells the same every day and smells like you? We are not talking about newlyweds here but couples who have been married for 25 or 10 or even 5 years.

For a marriage to be successful, couples must maintain an aura of interestingness. You must plan and strategize things to keep your bond strong, and it is best to start early. Restore the closeness between you before the attachment grows weak over time. Though it may seem trivial, it can create a large rift in your communication if you don't do this. One of you may end up being a silent sufferer, develop ill feelings, resentment or dissatisfaction, and nurture a grudge for being taken for granted. This leads to negativity and undermines mutuality. A greater disengagement is exhibited, and you end up communicating less and start avoiding each other's company.

Home is a place that puts our interpersonal skills to the test. By nature, men and women are different. Their needs, wants, and desires also vary. This difference between you will widen and grow if you cannot keep yourself interesting, if not just a little more interesting.

Women need more space for their toiletries and spend more time in front of the mirror. Partners need to allot separate space for their personal toiletries. This builds positive interaction, the continuation of bonding, and prevents the deterioration of the relationship. It brings harmony in your relationship and rules out all traces of disharmony. This is very essential to a loving, stable and enduring relationship.

NEVER STOP FORGIVING

One of the keys to having a happy relationship is to master the art of forgiving. It is an excellent quality and the towering virtue that every relationship must possess. In your relationship, there might come a time when the fire of love begins to dim, due to mistreatment and broken trust, leaving our hearts deeply wounded and bleeding. The virtue of forgiveness is that it is a great shield to lend you help during such times.

The sad truth is that some pain lingers on because we are not ready to forgive. Though we may try to forget and get over the pain, sometimes we feel that something is impossible to forgive. Pain has clouded our judgment and trust towards our partner. Our views and decisions become subjective, and we might not notice that we are already trapped in the vicious cycle of hurt and anger. Silently, this leads every relationship to an end.

To develop the virtue of forgiveness, we need to start by learning how to forgive ourselves. Forgiveness should start from within, and eventually we will learn how to forgive others, especially our partner. It takes time and courage to nurture, but when it is present, it will change our perception and insights. That will make it easier the next time someone asks for forgiveness, and hopefully the virtue will become habitual. Forgiving also makes us stronger and widens our understanding not just as a lover but as a person. So take the opportunity to learn lessons from your experiences. Gather your thoughts and attitudes - either the ones you have at the moment or ones from the past - and write them down in a journal. This will provide a safe and uncensored outlet for deeply held emotions.

Then begin to heal by forgiving. This develops our inner maturity and frees us from emotional bondage. Forgiveness means detaching yourself from past destructive behavior that has caused physical and emotional damage to others. It enables us to shake off a guilty conscience with firm determination not to repeat past misdeeds. Let us be gentle with ourselves and others. We should accept our own flaws and learn to improve ourselves by overcoming mistakes and failures.

Thus, make a commitment to forgive. Develop this virtuous trait purposefully. It will have added bonuses for us in the long run. Wisdom and experience tell us that we cannot change situations or the behavior of others. However, we do have control over our reaction to a given situation or challenge. It is just a matter of cultivating the right attitude. Develop empathy. And remember, to err is human and to forgive is divine. Do not bear a grudge or hatred towards any wrongdoer. Instead, respond with kindness to every mistake your partner makes. Prioritize showing forgiveness, even to the most unforgivable people. Though this is easier said than done, we must attempt it. It will free us from resentment, anxiety, depression and negativity. Furthermore, it will boost our emotional resilience. In the end, valuing the virtue of forgiveness is an indicator of our refined attitude towards life and its challenges.

Let forgiveness peacefully enter into your life and every relationship. It releases both parties from the pain of conflict. Do not allow yourself to become upset by catastrophes and nightmarish experiences. Instead, talk, understand and forgive each mistake made by your partner. Forgiveness doesn't just remove all negativity from a person, but it also saves worthwhile relationships. As such, the act of forgiving improves every relationship tremendously.

BONDING IN THE BATHROOM

Many marriages today are lackluster arrangements of companionship, devoid of the fragrance of love and comradeship. Though living under the same roof, the two partners may lead separate lives. It is time to bridge the gap and get rid of complacent behavior towards living with each other.

Expressing love is the best solution to this problem. It is a tried and tested means to vanquish both the physical and emotional distance. In romantic relationships, there is one special way to express your sincere love that guarantees enjoyment and magical results. It is bonding together in the bathroom.

There are three things that will help you to ensure happiness in your marriage and to make it through a marital crisis. The first thing is establishing a soothing friendship with one another. Only when there is companionship between partners can a more mature relationship arise wherein each individual is understanding and accepts his or her partner's flaws. For any marriage to succeed, there should be a relationship between equals. Secondly, respect towards one another is a must. The magic words in all successful relationships are: mutual respect. It should not be only a one-way road; it demands reciprocity. Give your partner the respect he or she deserves and command the respect you deserve. The third thing is trust. It is considered to be the golden rule in every relationship. This small yet powerful word can become the "make or break" factor in a relationship.

All of these three things can be enhanced through bonding together in the bathroom. It increases physical intimacy, and you can express love in an uninhibited fashion. There are no more secrets as you experience the bliss of romance and oneness. The act of bonding in the bathroom renews and adds life to your relationship. Through the physical love act, your hearts also blend as you respond to each other's needs and gestures. There will be greater love, respect and trust in your togetherness. It will leaves a trail of blazing love and energize you. You will feel intuitively drawn towards your partner for physical, mental and moral solace. Do not confine your love making to the bedroom alone; be innovative and explore each other in the bathroom too. Play Cupid and keeps the sparks alive by keeping communication channels open. Satiate your passion in all possible ways. This way you will feel fulfilled and complete as a person. Be honest with each other. Give yourself totally, with a carefree attitude, and win your lover forever. The chemistry that works in the bathroom will leave a lingering trail of love filled with togetherness.

When you love someone, you should express it openly through your words and deeds. Bonding in the bathroom is the surest way to keep togetherness fresh and the relationship lovely and lively. It is said that the stars in the sky can be counted and the drops in the ocean can be measured, but love, oh dear love cannot be measured. When we try to quantify love, we degrade it. We put a damper on its endlessness. Love is like the sky. It has no end. True love speaks less and says more. It is overwhelming, and it overwhelms the other person. Love is to be felt, experienced and shared. Its true essence is to be imbibed. Any attempt to quantify love decreases its greatness. Hail the power of love and savor it by bonding in the bathroom.

SHARE YOUR PARTNER'S PAINS AND PLEASURES

How would you rate your relationship with your partner? Is it bad, routine or the best? Are you cheerful with each other or do you engage in verbal assaults? Do you take each other for granted?

Marriage is a blessing, but when handled poorly it turns into a nightmare. Your desire for a deep, intense, and conflict-free relationship will become a reality when you willingly share your partner's pains and pleasures. Having a sense of shared purpose and the quality of your friendship are the keys to unlock harmonious and everlasting marital bliss. Both partners must treat all problems and blessings as "ours." Let each other feel that you have one another to lean on at all times. Marriage is all about love, trust, sharing and friendship. Share all the ups and downs of life with the true spirit of a long-standing life partnership.

Marriage is an arrangement between equals with mutual trust and respect. It is sprinkled with love, appreciation and understanding. Consequently, being in a marriage will improve your vibes.

In sharing every piece of what you have with your partner, use common sense to avoid "potholes" and always have clarity in your approach to avoid misunderstandings. When things get heated, step away for a moment. You must be aware that by managing your anger, you are indirectly managing his/her anger too. Be open to each other and correct each other respectfully without demeaning one another's worth.

Disassociate from negative emotions and maintain a positive attitude. Remember, you share these feelings with each other, so if you fill your heart with anger, your partner's heart will be filled with it too. Always bear in mind that every action has consequences, so think twice and reflect before acting. Be the change you wish to see in him or her. Love and respect need to be earned by one's own behavior and not forced. Learn to harmonize your life around each other to minimize differences. There must be total trust and commitment with no room, if possible, for suspicion and mistrust.

Couples who share the pains and pleasures of day-to-day life can counsel and support each other and minimize their grievances. With will power and cooperation, pain can be turned into pleasure. Marital relationships should be actively managed by working on them and constantly renewing them. Be your partner's emotional anchor. Be each other's strength by sharing all your pain and pleasure with one another.

Proof

31822423R00090

Made in the USA
Charleston, SC
26 July 2014